Shades of Faith
Minority Voices Within Paganism

Edited by Crystal Blanton

Contributing authors include
Crystal Blanton
Luisah Teish
Luna Pantera
Iyanifa Onifa Karade
Heaven Walker
Olivia Haynes
Flame Bridhesdottir
Nadirah Adeye
Gloria Jean
Storm Kelly
Szmeralda Shanel
Yvonne Nieves
Leilani Birley
La Pixie (Sandra Posadas)
Yonv Unega
Uzuri Amini (Ishe Fa'lona Oshun Iya Oshogbo)
Anniitra Makafia UtchatiNu Ravenmoon
Janet Callahan
K.W.
Lilith Silverkrow

Shades of Faith
Minority Voices Within Paganism

Edited by Crystal Blanton

Megalithica Books

Stafford, England

Shades of Faith: Minority Voices Within Paganism
Edited by Crystal Blanton
© 2011 Crystal Blanton and individual contributors

Cover Photograph: Crystal Blanton
Photograph Model: Melissa Kennedy
Cover Design: Angelique Mroczka
Editor: Crystal Blanton
Layout: Taylor Ellwood

Set in Book Antiqua

First Edition 2011

MB0151

ISBN 978-1-905713-69-1

A Megalithica Books Publication
An imprint of Immanion Press
http://www.immanion-press.com
info@immanion-press.com

8 Rowley Grove
Stafford ST17 9BJ
UK

Table of Contents

When you're a little kid, you don't see color, and the fact that my friends were black never crossed my mind. It never became an issue until I was a teenager and started trying to rap.
Eminem

I don't stand for the black man's side; I don't stand for the white man's side. I stand for God's side.
Bob Marley

I realize that I'm black, but I like to be viewed as a person, and this is everybody's wish.
Michael Jordan

I'm black, I don't feel burdened by it and I don't think it's a huge responsibility. It's part of who I am. It does not define me.
Oprah Winfrey

The Black skin is not a badge of shame, but rather a glorious symbol of national greatness.
Marcus Garvey

Introduction

Crystal Blanton

My black face, my red beating heart.

I am many things and I am comprised of many pieces. All of my parts bring together a wholeness, no longer able to be separated from the elements within the creation. Each and every part of me has contributed to who I have become and who I may become in the future. I am a woman, an American, a wife, sister, daughter, mother, author, counselor, friend, auntie, teacher and a healer. Did I mention I am also Black and a Wiccan High Priestess? All of these parts of myself have been polished with time and there will be more elements to go through the polishing process and incorporate into the wholeness of my being.

I was raised mostly by my single mother in the San Francisco Bay Area in a mostly Caucasian town. I was one of three or four Black kids in my entire elementary school until about fifth or sixth grade. My mother was from the south, which is normal for Black families on the west coast, and most of our family were still in the south. I was raised to appreciate diversity and to be surrounded by a variety of people who looked different than me. I was conditioned to be different than others, often being the only black person in any given social setting.

This did not bother me growing up; it was normal for me. It was not until my adulthood that I realized how different I was from those who may have been raised surrounded by others of their birth culture. It was not surprising that I married without a thought of race and landed within the Pagan community.

I went through reading about parts of my Americanized heritage and the oppression that was caused. I became obsessed for a while with the history of the Black Panther Party for Self Defense and love the history of my culture. As I have continued to grow within my spiritual self, I have been able to see the incredible importance of, once again, being the minority within the majority. There is beauty in the rose colored glasses of my ancestry and a direct lineage of some of the most powerful people to ever survive and live in this world. I have no reason to doubt the immense power running through my veins and the experience of divine power that inspired a whole culture of people to continue to move forward despite conditions that were unimaginable. This internal knowledge has served me quite well in my journey to spiritual awareness.

What appears to be conflicting elements between being raised away from my community and being infused into the culture of Paganism where I am the black face, actually fit together in many ways. I am accustomed to being who I am among those who are different. I am also accustomed to seeing the world a little differently because my experiences in the world are different. I am used to being the one that people have turned to when they wanted to ask a question about cultures outside of their own. This has become a part of what I recognize as a gift the Gods have graced me with; and like the pattern of my life, I have found a path to purpose in being the minority within the minority.

Recognizing the path to being Pagan or Wiccan usually starts with an infiltration of images with Greek and Celtic Gods, images of flowing hair and fair skin. The Egyptian pantheon is the only darker pigmentation pantheon that walks the fine line of acceptability in Wiccan culture. Unclear of why this is, I have always wondered why Egyptian culture has been more mainstream acceptable than African or even African American. It has often occurred to me that engaging in the study of the history of Egyptians is more comfortable for some people when they do not have to refer to them as they are; African. In a culture that has often celebrated lighter skin, American culture (which means White) and with a history of "white is right" types of mentality, separating the Egyptians from African makes it easier to accept their culture as approachable and fascinating.

It was my journey of studying the "acceptable" or commonly discussed deities within Wicca that led me to a journey of exploration that ended with a need to work within the African Diaspora. I cannot explain why but they called to me before I had to chance to look for them. As much as I adore the Egyptian pantheon, I do not work with them as my Patron or Matron. Nor was I claimed by the Celtic, Greek/Roman or Norse. The blood of my ancestors connected me to a lineage rich in knowledge and the voice of Yemaya called from the Sea and the King of the white cloth, Obatala, rose from the heavens.

Not only did I find myself as a Black, Wiccan High Priestess; now I found that I was joined to the power of the African Gods. Talk about a mixture of eclecticism.

In writing about my path of being a minority voice within Paganism, I don't feel disheartened. I feel blessed to share my culture with others and to learn their cultures from them. As the black face among the crowd I have had to adapt to my surroundings and find a way to exist within them. I have had to find a way to build community without the commonality of heritage but with the love of the Gods that come to us in many forms and whisper with different tongues. This blessing has allowed me to find oneness with my own deities while connecting to the divineness of others. Is this not one of the true lessons of spiritual knowledge in its finest?

Whether I call to Hecate in ritual or to Gaia, I am a walking manifestation of divine spirit within this coat of darkened skin with full lips and round hips. I carry the wisdom of ancestors who were Pagans at birth, worshiping and living from the land in all of its splendor. I cannot separate my blackness from being Wiccan, nor would I want to. Both sides of me are intertwined in a delicate dance of pride that call this mind and this body home. My home travels with me, as do my ancestors and my Gods.

Often I hear of stories of alienation within the community from those who look as I do. I understand it and do not attribute that to the path of Wicca or Paganism. I attribute it to the path of being a minority, African American, Black, colored, dark skinned human being. Too often it is associated with pain and not often enough is it looked at as the unexpected treasure of adversity. In my world I know I have a voice that is seldom heard and the world suffers from the lack of shared knowledge of any culture. Togetherness brings power to any community; Paganism is no different. The voice of differences add an element of harmony to the collective voices of any path or movement. We are in the human and social movement of spiritual understanding; Black, White, Hispanic, Native or other. Together we harmonize on a frequency that is powerful enough to manifest divinity on earth and bring spiritual rest to so much collective suffering and pain. I am honored to be the black key on the piano.

Cultural awareness brings about social change. This anthology gives an unprecedented opportunity for the often underrepresented minority voice to be heard within the confines of Pagan experience and thought. There are more minorities entering Paganism everyday and culturally we are finding the rhythm between the expectations of our birth culture and that of the Pagan community; it is a dance of great importance. In order to sustain our community we have to grow towards the acknowledgement of all things sacred within our path. Whether that is methods of practice, skin color, sexuality or residing country; all are welcome in the land of the God and Goddess.

May this anthology give you an understanding of the many experiences and delicate dilemmas of being the minority within the minority. As some of the experiences in this book bring about personal stories of the uncomfortable moments, others will bring about feelings of culture and celebration. As we say in drug and alcohol treatment, we are to understand rather than be understood. May this book support a culture within Paganism of just that, collective understanding among the diversity of this wonderful community of celebration and faith.

Multicolored Momma

Originally printed in Jambalaya by Luisha Teish and reprinted with
permission

My sweet coffee skin
Hold secrets in its shade,
Whispers silent warning
To a black and white world

Do not box me in
In your narrow racial jackets,
Too tight to move in,
Too thin to wear.

My brown pores bleed
With the sweat of many nations,
Generations of colors
Ooze down my arm.

My Bantu behind
Plays the drums of dancing griots,
Telling stories with my sway
Singing songs with each step.

My high Choctaw cheekbones
Love the Mississippi Delta.
Remembers Running Cloud's daughter
And the Red Man gone.

My breast angle 'round
Like the dark gypsy wenches.
Crescent moons touch my belly
Silver slithers on my throat.

My almond eyes sparkle
To the sound of Eastern jingles
Glass chimes dress my eyelids
Tinkling bells kiss my brow.

Luisha Teish

My dirty red hair
Speaks of crazy Cajun cousins,
Talks of faire Creole ladies
And their dark Spanish men.

My Tibetan thighs open
And the Red Sea splits.
My soft lips part
Between Dahomey and Brazil.

My sweet coffee skin
Holds secrets in its shade,
Whispers silent warnings
To a black and white world.

I will not wear
Your narrow racial jackets
As the blood of many nations
Runs sweetly thru my veins.

Coming Out of the Closet

Crystal Blanton

In my eyes I am whole,
I know how to heal my soul.
I am one with the universe and blessed with her grace
I have found myself and things have fallen into place

I now understand….I can see
I feel the changing of the seasons inside of me
Maiden, Mother, Crone…. inside of me I feel
Season's change with each turn of the wheel

I feel the spirit in my heart
I see the god in the trees
I feel the goddess in the breeze
I am rejuvenated by water's embrace
My blood warms with fire's grace

I know I have been here before,
I know I will come again,
A place for me waits in Summerland

I am a woman, I am a mother,
I am a daughter, I am a sister,
I am a friend,
I am a goddess……..
I am a witch

Don't Be Afraid of the Dark

Iyanifa Onifa Karade

The fear of the dark, the other, the outside, the unknown infuses my pagan experience.

Be it looking for gathering places in the "alternative" community or patiently explaining to people that I will not set a curse for them against their enemies; It's the same story over and over again; a brown woman who professes to love voodoo and practice it is a bit unnerving. For every tentative contact I receive from the non-voodoo practicing Pagan community there are three more asking if one must be of African descent to attend gatherings or if we will be sacrificing animals and if so, they are strongly against it.

This type of overt racism would be bemusing if it weren't so sincere, so pristine in its appearance.

And it all goes back to a fear of the Dark. The other. Those people. Them. They.

So my biggest work in the community is embodying the principle of releasing the fear of the dark because if you are afraid of what goes bump in the night you are ultimately afraid of me, 'cause I'm out there. Candle in hand, draped in white, head tied, whispering a Yoruba song, speaking to the Mothers as I cast about for a good place to leave an offering in the woods. I'm the person you sneak to contact when the fertility drugs have failed you and your faith in medicine is weak. When the noises you hear from the basement every full moon become too much to bear, and the tarot reader at the crystal healing bookstore shrinks away from the fear in your eyes. When your son hears voices that tell him to drum and speaks of a Grandmother you never knew who teaches him how to read the stars every night when he goes to bed. When the chest of drawers you got from the estate sale, remember the one that was such a steal, starts to move around on its own whenever you leave home. When the former residents of your home refuse to move on to the other side and peek at you from cracks in your bedroom closet door.

You call me, cause I'm not afraid of the dark.

I'm not afraid to patiently explain the transatlantic slave trade for the hundredth time in an hour when people seem perplexed to see me seriously undertaking the religious beliefs of my Ancestors. I'm ok when I have to hear about how much you fear animal sacrifice but love chicken and family barbecues. I have to hear how "dark" voodoo is, as if darkness is to be avoided at all costs, as if the womb is a bad place to have come from...or to return to. I have to hear about how you've always been interested in "that stuff" after you saw it on a movie and wanted to know more. I get to explain how voodoo is really Vodoun when you treat it with respect, capitalize that small "v", and give us the same respect you give your own spiritual path. I repeat unceasingly the connection between Santeria, Haitian Vodou, Obeah, conjure, Palo, Ifa, Akan, West African Voudoun. I get to hear you tell me how I'm all mixed up, that I couldn't possibly be practicing New Orleans Voodoo along with Ifa while hollering at Lucero and Sarabanda to keep the noise down on the back porch. I get to hear how I'm supposed to ignore the Native blood that runs in my veins and the Spirits of the Native Stewards of the land that I walk on because I don't look Indian enough for you.

I get to do all of that and then talk to you about your fear of the dark. Because that's all it is. A fear of the dark; the unknown, the murky dusky places in the psyche where truth dwells and the only light that you may find will be within your own mind. I get to hear how little I know about who I am because you know more, and you know for sure that there couldn't possibly be any philosophical underpinnings to such a savage act as blessing an animal before releasing its spirit and eating it with my family. This is what I get to do when I leave my home and venture out into the Pagan community and draw a veve on my table before I do readings that require sacrifice. Sacrifice of the desire to consume more than one needs, to hoard rather than share, to defy rather than to cooperate, to stumble rather than to fly. I get to hear you express your fears about who I am and what I am doing in the dark when out of your sight.

I have been practicing what folk call Paganism my entire life and only recognized it as such at 18 years old when I began to look for the Goddess that looked like me and no one knew who She was. After finding Her, She's been finding me ever since. When I practiced Wicca I thought that acknowledging elements and honoring the celebratory days on wheel of the year would satisfy my cravings to reconnect with Earth energy. It gave me a taste of something that I just couldn't identify. It was if I were hungry and could smell a banquet of delicious foods somewhere in the vicinity...and just couldn't seem to locate where it was. I added prayers to the Kemetic and Yoruba Orisha in my Wicca practice, and that wasn't it either. There was just something missing, something too mild, too accommodating. I perceived a fear of power, Christian God/Dess wearing a pentacle instead of a cross. A lot of fear of the unknown, fear of mastering oneself, fear of the Other, fear of releasing oneself from bondage and fear of honoring one's ancestors, of working with the dead. There was definitely a phobia of anything African in nature. You know, Voodoo. That was dark. Worked with negative forces, it should be avoided at all costs.

Every time I heard that tagline I felt as if I were being told to ignore me, the woman in the mirror and reach for blond Artemis or Aphrodite. I came to learn that I was being steered away from the Indigenous spirituality of people who looked like me to look at deities who didn't.

It felt a bit like Jesus camp; same message, same vibe. Anything that looks like me is...evil? Wrong? Ignore the historical atrocities, dance the spiral dance and merry meet and merry part and...

It didn't gel. It just didn't add up for me. Something that my soul hungered for and my spirit craved was missing.

I released practicing Wicca when I found Vodoun. It was then that I knew I'd come home. I received initiations in a few different African Spiritual Systems because my Ancestors called for me to do it. I answer the call of the spirits and allow them to take me home so my unknown Ancestors can have a voice and be fed and elevated. As a Iyanifa, Sistah Servant of the Spirits, Kongo Spiritwomon ,I teach, guide, write, interview, edit, and sing about another way of life, one that can exist right here along with you, where you can come to learn the nature of the universe and your role in it. I tell people to stop being afraid of the dark. I tell them if they can eliminate that fear, and face it head on that they will be able to go into their darkness to find the light. I say how too much light can be blinding and that all things have a purpose and place within the Universe, even the darkness. How racist it is to use the term "darkness" when referring to negativity, which is really only one step away from just saying "darkie" when talking about me or people who look like me.

The biggest hindrance toward more acceptance in the Pagan community for me is that I'm not looking for it; I'm simply living out my Destiny, which at times calls for me to enter the world at a certain place and time doing certain things in certain ways. Sometimes acceptance finds me, sometimes it doesn't. I live by a code that requires me to deal with whatever hand I'm dealt in a way that leaves me with more grace, awareness, patience, and composure than what I started off with. It is a code of honor, and within that honor there is no place for seeking acceptance in the way that is currently in vogue. I would say that offering acceptance is more in alignment with the code I live by and if it is returned, that is wonderful and if it isn't, that is wonderful too.

I look forward to seeing a convergence of resources from many different Pagan traditions in relationship to finding methods that "work", that get results in this strange new world we are facing in the 21st century. This world is going to require a lot from us all: witches, warlocks, bokors, hougans, priestesses, mamissi ,and hounsi. The requirements to survive are still being revealed, the costs are still high. What our collective Ancestors needed to survive over 100 years ago isn't exactly what we need today, at least not materially. What they had spiritually we need desperately. It is time to revisit, reawaken, and reconstitute what we need to thrive daily, weekly, and monthly not only for us but for leaving a legacy to our children, both by birth and spirit. We have the privilege of having lived through the changing of a century movement from the industrial age to the dawn of the information age. We have a lot to share and a lot to discard just so we don't accidentally leave the wrong experience with our children. We have an opportunity to forge a real new age of clarity, peace, laughter, and song, and I don't intend to let it pass me by.

For that reason alone it is worth me telling the same story repeatedly because sometimes, in many ways, people are just trying to remember who they are and who their Ancestors have called them to be.

It is the simple stories that work best, so it is with them that I will stay and continue to teach the people as I was charged to do to return to tradition and the ways of the Ancestors.

In the Spirit of Alafia: Many Paths for Many People

Luisha Teish

In keeping with my practice as an Orisha priestess and a Goddess worshipper, I will begin with a greeting to the village and an acknowledgement of some of the women who have supported me on my journey.

Now I say " Alafia." Alafia is a Yoruba greeting granting that you have good health and be at peace with your neighbor. Your response is "Sha Alafia ni" which returns the blessing to me.

Let us consider for a moment what our lives could be like if we truly lived in good health and were at peace with our neighbors. It would mean a better life for us all.

There are many women who have guided me in finding my spiritual path and living a better life. Among them I pay homage to: My Mother, Serena Scott Allen who brought me into this world and sacrificed her life for mine. To her mother Mary Jones Scott, to her Mother Rachel Squaw Jones and to her mother Running Cloud.

My second grade teacher Mrs. Gladys Gibson who called me " her pretty little genius" and whose voice echoes in my head even today. Mrs. Joyce Combs Abrams, my writing teacher who helped me to chose the right road. Ms. Joan Bailey, my high school dance teacher who sat me on the path to beauty.

To the Women's Society of Ile Orunmila Oshun whose dedication, love and courage regenerates our tradition.

And to the Women of All Traditions who dare to stand up to patriarchal oppression.

Love and Respect to You.

I'm standing in front of a group of Black People at a library in Berkeley, Ca. Or maybe it's that college I used to attend, or that theater where I sometimes perform. It could be any number of places where I am a member of a panel discussing Black Culture and Spirituality, art activism, or environmental justice issues.

Usually there are a number of people from different spiritual traditions in the room. This is especially important if the majority of people are African-Americans. In a room full of Black people the majority are bound to be Christians, followed by Moslems, Kemetic-Egyptians, and a few black Hebrews. Often there is an undercurrent of class division and spiritual dominance. Often the tension exists between these groups because each believes (and maybe even insists) that their God is "the only true God."

Inside my head I hear "My god's bigger than your god, my god's bigger than yours" sung to the tune of a dog-food commercial (Ken-L-Ration).

In this gathering, there may be a few people who have followed the path of Buddhist contemplation or found their home in Native American Earth Reverence. There is a growing number of African-American women who embrace the "Dark Goddess", and even some Christians can manage to utter the phrase "God the Mother."

This census of mine grows smaller as I count the people who practice Ifa/Orisha, Voudoun, Akan, Mysticism and New Thought traditions. These people are regarded as "pagans" by the monotheist. I smile to myself because I've practiced just about all of these traditions during my lifetime.

You might wonder how on Earth I became this kind of person.

The background of my life as a child growing up tipsy in New Orleans and the road I took to arrive on my spiritual path is best understood by reading the first few chapters of my book "Jambalaya: The Natural Woman's Book of Personal Charms and Practical Rituals".

Although the book is written from an African-American cultural perspective and honors the spiritual power of women, it addresses some of our most common human experiences.

The many twist and turns, the trials and triumphs of my youth can be understood by anyone who has experienced growing up with a hunger for spirituality rather than religion.

Each and every one of us has a contract with Creation. We all came here to be somebody, to do something important, and to have the best life it's possible for us to have this lifetime. Whatever traditions and spiritual practices we choose should serve the fulfillment of our Contract with Creation. The road to my present level of spiritual development has been an exciting one.

Like most of us, my life began with innocence. I was a bare foot nappy headed little girl who looked at the world around me, and asked " how did things get to be the way they are, and why on earth am I on Earth?" The search for an answer to those questions led me to study several traditions and to take initiation in a few.

I had been christened African Methodist Episcopal in deference to the rites of my father's family, but my mother's policy was "God by any means necessary". This meant that I could go to any accessible church irrespective of the denomination. So I went to the Holiness, Baptist, Sanctified and other Protestant churches in whatever neighborhoods I found myself.

Then an important change occurred. My mother informed me that I had to "become Catholic" in order to fulfill a deathbed promise she'd made to her father.

By now my family had moved from New Orleans proper to a subdivision for colored people on the West Bank of the Mississippi River. Saint Rosalie, the local Catholic Church was segregated and "the children of Cain" were forbidden to pass through its doors. I tried to attend St. Rosalie's once and got chased across the tracks by little white boys with big sticks and stones.

So, she enrolled me in a Catholic School (All Saints) in Algiers, Louisiana, two towns away because this was the closest Catholic Church that admitted Black people.

As a good little Catholic girl, I was devoted to the Virgin Mary.

I loved the incense and fancy robes, communion and the rituals of midnight mass on Christmas Eve and Sunrise service on Easter.

I studied the catechism, sang the Requiem, and worked in the convent. Yet there were things about the church that bothered me. In catechism class I was required to pray for the conversion of the Jews. And my mother had worked for a very nice Jewish lady (a Mrs. Lichtenstein) and I didn't see nothing wrong with her.

My mother couldn't take communion because she had married a Protestant man. And worst of all I found out that the Catholic Church had sponsored the African slave trade.

So, I began to actively question the nuns and the bible, and to challenge segregation in the church. I found a history of witch burning, invasion and enslavement. I realized that I had to abandon it and search for something that supported my growth as a whole human being.

Investigating my ancestry led me to readings on the Ancestor Reverence and Nature Worship practices of West Africa.

In recognition of my mother's mother, I have participated, (respectfully), in Native American ceremonies such as sweat lodge and medicine wheel.

When I learned of the glory of Egypt, I was initiated into the Mysteries of Isis and Hathor.

My primary spiritual identity is as a priestess of Oshun, the Yoruba Goddess of Love, Art, and Sensuality. Upon receiving Oshun, I became very clear that my assignment in this life was to bring joy and beauty into the world in a spiritual context; and to help others find that sacredness within themselves, in nature and in spirit.

Through the gracious sharing by some of my Wiccan sisters, I have been invited to partake of pre-patriarchal European rites and ceremonies. I face the East through devotionals to Pele, the Green Tara, Laksmi, and Quan Yin.

In addition, I am an Iyanifa. Now as soon as I say, " I am Iyanifa" a clamor may be heard. Some women in Yoruba tradition will stand up and cheer in honor of the complementary relationship between Destiny (Ifa) and Love (Oshun). Others (most probably men) will claim that Ifa, the highest level of the priesthood, is reserved exclusively for men, and that no such woman exists. In response, I can only offer the wisdom of a proverb from the Holy Yoruba Orature: **"The person who knows does not die in the same manner as those who do not know."**

I have been a student of spiritual cultures most of my life. As I look back on the sequence of events in my life its seems to me that I've always known there was a different truth, a different perspective, a different story to be told. As early as Elementary school, I found myself reacting to the lies told about Eve and Pandora. Somehow, I realized that the strong Black women I grew up with (my mother, aunts and neighbors) were reflections of the Feminine face of God.

My studies support my hope and belief. It is my sincere hope that we, humans, are evolving toward a non-competitive Eco-spiritual perspective that will allow us to see each other as children of a common Mother, Earth, with a common Father, Spirit. And these parents rejoice in the diversity and beauty of Their children.

African Americans have, I feel, a particular assignment at this point in our history. As Africans, we are the fore parents of humanity and we have a right to practice any and every tradition created by Our Children, the humans. As Americans we are conditioned to a sense of entitlement (based on material wealth rather than good character), and at the same time we are often denied access to the resources that would allow us to practice our spirituality our way. It is important that we stand tall and brave, that we study diligently and celebrate joyously, that we remember the past as we create the future. All the while, we must remain humble and be true to ourselves and our place in the world.

I pray for and hold a vision of a future in which we will:

1. Liberate ourselves from fundamentalism (which rules by fear/guilt and stifles growth)
2. Reclaim our ancestral deities.
3. Heal from racism, sexism, and erosphobia. (These are at the heart of most intra-cultural disruptions).
4. Renew our relationship to the natural world.
5. Integrate both God and Goddess into our daily lives.

In short, it is my prayer that we will heal from internalized oppression so we can face and overcome any onslaught from without.

Blessed be you, your ancestors and your children.

In the Spirit,
Luisah Teish

Shedding in Creation

Nadirah Adeye

I was 18 years old, just weeks from my high school graduation, when Goddess came to me in a dream and claimed me as Her own. I have since come to recognize these dream-time events as more than dreaming; my spirit was night traveling.

She was the most beautiful being I had ever seen, petite and brown, wearing a bright red and gold dress and veil. She was surprisingly small, reaching up to me, cupping my cheeks in the warmth of Her hands and tilting my face so She could look into my eyes. I was resistant, afraid of what was coming, as She covered me with a black and white veil in which I would be taken away. I woke up feeling touched, seen, and loved in a way that has deeply affected my life in the years since that night.

At the time of the dream it had been six years since I'd started refusing to attend church with my mother. I had been studying Goddess-related history for almost four years, reading everything I could purchase or order through my local library branch. It had been nine years since I'd fervently promised the Creator that I would commit my life to the Spiritual path "if only I could just be a little girl for now." My reprieve had lasted for five years.

Today, I am a priestess whose life is committed to being a student of and a vessel for the Divine. I am a hereditary practitioner from a family that has always had a strong connection to the Creator. I feel blessed and privileged to have inherited that connection. I have seen the power of God working in the lives of my relatives and feel that, though my path and practice has a different name, our work is much the same. I believe that, no matter the time or place my family incarnates, we are the ones who open the gates to other worlds for our communities- through words, song, dance, service, listening and connection.

I am an ordained Priestess of the CAYA Amazon Dianic Tradition. I am a graduate of one of the few Women's Spirituality Master's Degree programs in the world. I am a priestess member and student of the Iseum of Black Isis. I am a student of the Feri tradition. I have sat and prayed in lodges, I chant, I sit, I trance, meditate, sing, dance, cast spells, and make sex magick. I am a daughter of Auset, Yemaya rules my head, and Oshun is one of my honey aunties. I have been trained by Goddess Herself and by priests and priestesses in Her service. My first and most important relationship is with Goddess and it is the filter through which all of my other relationships flow.

Writing an article on being a woman of color in the pagan community at this time in my life feels ironic and strange for a number of reasons. I've recently decided I no longer wish to act as a black ambassador to an unconscious white world. At the same time I've recently reached a place of understanding of how it might feel to transcend ethnic identity. I recognize, and am amused by, the contradiction of those two statements. I've also recently decided that I would like to receive my spiritual nourishment through ritual work in circle with other African American female priestesses whose magick I know and trust. It seems that my world has simultaneously narrowed and expanded. My intention in this article is to stand a moment in this place of contradiction that defines my current existence. I am living, consciously, at the center of an energetic mill- hibernating, shedding and creating all at once.

About five years ago, I began working in the field of diversity, seeking personal growth and transformation. As a person of color in non-traditional spiritual settings, I was frequently one of the only or one of the few non-white participants. I will not spell out the details of my experiences; they are my own, and I am sure that any person of color who has been in a similar position has plenty of their own memories to draw from. I loved that ritual offered a place where we could shed our skins and their stories and receive the nurturance and nourishment that our spirits needed. Unfortunately, I found that cultural insensitivity will show up in space deemed sacred as readily as it does in secular space. And disappointingly, I found that, many white pagans say things like "So-and-so calls us regardless of race or skin color" to explain worshiping deities of color and/or adopting the sacred practices of traditional indigenous peoples. But when the conversations turn to things like spiritual bypassing (using spirituality to avoid directly addressing challenging realities facing us) or appropriation (taking something created by others and making it one's own, sometimes out of context) then communication shuts down and defenses rise.

I wanted to find a way to speak to the uncomfortable situations that I encountered in these spaces. I wanted to find a way to stop being polite about unacceptable unconscious offenses. I *really* wanted to find a way that I could stop feeling threatened when I was going places to pray. I was determined to stop feeling assaulted at church.

I began working at an organization that offered trainings and education in racism/sexism/homophobia/classism and how to unlearn the patterns and behaviors that go along with them. I found that, while increasing my ability to give voice to the pain I felt from negative encounters, I was also learning to listen to the impact I had when acting from my own lack of awareness. I also learned to recognize some of the common and subtle ways in which people exhibit and defend their prejudice without realizing it. Things like stereotyping, resistance to hearing the effect their unconscious comments can have on others, becoming defensive and argumentative, expressing hostility, turning the conversation to their own cultural (or gender or sexual orientation) experience to prove they are not racist or homophobic or sexist. I also learned to see that people were doing a lot of these things in an attempt to prove that they are not bad people. That awareness helped me to develop compassion for myself and others in those uncomfortable, unpleasant moments.

I moved from there to another organization where I would have daily opportunities to practice what I'd learned while also addressing my own mistrust of white people. I took a job at a spiritual organization where diversity was one of their greatest challenges. According to the 2000 census, 94% of the population in the local community identified themselves as white. On the staff, I was one of only three people of color and was the only one who was American born. (I make this distinction because I have found that the various and subtle ways prejudices interact and impact each other can be challenging for people who immigrate to the US as adults to understand.)

It was transformative for me to immerse myself in the culture of this organization for the time I was there. I witnessed a lot of unskillful behaviors. I also made a lot of mistakes and was not always my best self. One of the greatest lessons I have taken from the experience is this: The teacher who is unwilling to learn from and be changed by her students is a teacher who has made a willful decision to arrest her growth. The temple whose leadership is resistant to change (whether in themselves or in their organization), the church that is set in certain ways of being, despite negative feedback from its congregation, the spiritual center that is only effective for a certain community, is one that will age and die with its leadership no matter how beautiful the works being done within. Being a priest or priestess and standing in the flow of the Divine means, at times, changing or shedding in ways that may be uncomfortable or not according to our personal plans.

After years of personal work and numerous missteps, I have come to a place of relative peace around white spiritual practitioners in the Bay Area. The result of which is that I have realized that my drive to work in the field of diversity and my feeling that it is the route for my work as a priestess, is gone, at least for the moment. I strongly believe that it is every person's responsibility to educate themselves and share what they know with those around them. When it comes to matters of racism, though, it is white people's responsibility to educate each other about race, racism, and the accompanying power dynamics. I continue to speak to what I witness in a space and am fortunate, because of my work of the last several years, to be able to recommend some amazing resources for people who are in need. Beyond that I have decided that, for now, I will not expend energy on futile efforts or outside of my personal, spiritual, and familial communities.

I have been fortunate to be able to attend three week-long, silent meditative Vipassana retreats in the last couple of years. From them, I have learned that it is absolutely imperative that we have moments of inner quiet and stillness- those are the times when we can most clearly hear the wisdom that Creation has to offer us. The experiences of these retreats have been the greatest influence in my personal transformation of the last two years. It was on one of these retreats that I reached a place and a moment of understanding how it might feel to transcend my identity as an African American woman. I knew myself as a whole being, free of the psychic armor I wore on a daily basis to protect myself. I had heard these same ideas that we are not our bodies or our identities from teachers before, but they had rung false when expressed by people that I knew were hiding behind whiteness in resistance of an expanded diversity consciousness.

It is also as a result of attending those meditative retreats that I am realizing the importance of my current state- hibernation. I gave birth to my first child five months ago and, in preparation, I entered a space of retreat. I allowed myself to shed as much of the world as possible by slowing down, turning my focus more inward, looking at myself and my life and receiving the wisdom offered by reflection. This was an easy change to make when I was awaiting his birth, feeling lethargic and cumbersome. I felt that I was in an alchemical process, learning the lessons of Hathor/Isis, in her role as mother of Horus, the Mother whose name means "House of Horus." I was learning what it meant to literally be someone else's home- to have another being completely dependent on me for food and nourishment. I was very aware that even my emotional state affected him and his well-being.

Hibernation has been less easy to maintain in the months since the birth of my son. I've found that I am having to re-learn everything that I've done before. Taking stock of myself and my entire life to determine, "Am I continuing to walk a path that is true to me and who I am now? Am I living a life that is true to the goals I have for myself as a priestess, woman, mother, lover?" I am vividly aware that someone else will be watching me and my partner as we live our lives and I wonder- what are the lessons I'll be teaching him without realizing it?

I am living The Hermit card from the Tarot. Because of that fact, I have had to change what I respect as being productive. Where before it meant completing a list of goals or tasks and moving toward signs of success in the world. In the last months I have been learning to accept that (as one priestess friend put it) "If the baby is alive at the end of the day, I've done my job." This is all more challenging than I would have ever thought before. Moving slowly and accomplishing what seems to be only a few tasks in a day is hard for me to accept. I am helped by the fact that I am also seeing more subtle layers to my spiritual practice. Rousing and energizing ecstatic ritual practices have been temporarily replaced by the quieter and less obviously entertaining rituals of caring for my home, meal preparation, and baby nurturing. It's another state of contradiction. Even as this hibernation period and caring for my son seem to be taking me from the life I lived before, having him is showing me how important it is to one day turn my focus back outward- to continue finding ways to effect change in the world through my work, my words and my actions so that I can make the world a little better for him.

One of the challenges I felt about attempting to write this article was- Do I write about being black and pagan and detail how my blackness and spiritual path inform this writing? Or do I just choose to write my experience and know that since I am black and pagan, what I say is contributing to the story of what it means to be a person of color and a practitioner of non-standard spirituality? I have chosen the latter in a new attempt to write to and for only those who would understand my experience because it is, in some way, similar to their own.

Moving forward, with the awareness of where I have been and where I am currently standing, the question I am challenging myself to answer is *What is the nature of my magick and what is its purpose?* I've spent the last several years feeling as though I was trying to attain a certain degree of skill and personal awareness before being capable of turning my efforts outward in service to my communities. My intention when participating in ritual, chanting, meditation and lodges is always to emerge cleansed of the spiritual and energetic debris that accumulates from daily life. It is possible, but significantly more challenging, to recharge in a space where I feel the need to keep my shields up in protection against possible moments of cultural insensitivity. For that reason, I have realized that it is imperative to my work as a priestess to receive spiritual nourishment in settings with other women of color, where there is reliable support due to commonality of certain experiences and understanding.

I believe it is of vital importance to find and share our individual special skills in the world. I also believe that it is imperative that we know ourselves intimately enough to say with clarity "This is work that I can do, this is service that I will offer, these are skills that I do have." as well as being able to say and stand firm in saying "This will not work for me, this is what I will not accept, this is a deal breaker and I will not participate in it." Beyond that, it is critical that, once we know these things about ourselves, we have the courage to stand by them and to live our lives according to their truth.

My name is Nadirah Adeye and I am a priestess of Auset, the Black Mother, the glittering black void. Yemaya rules my head, Sekhmet/Hathor is my mother/teacher, and Oshun is one of my honey aunties. I walk the Third Path, the Middle Road, sitting and sweating to revitalize my spirit.

I have been a priestess, witch, conjurer, seeker on this path for over half of my life. I have always known my life would be committed to God. Though I did not know I would be given numerous opportunities to meet Her in many of Her ten thousand names! My life is one of richness, intensity, alchemy, sweet nectar, joy and bliss, ambition, growth, discipline, power, struggle and reward. I manifest with blessed skill and ease, and am humbled by the beauty of the gifts I have been given. I am blessed in life, in love, in talent and in wealth; and I strive, daily, to be a great representative of the Goddess in the world.

Invoking the Queen

Heaven Walker

Introduction

I began the journey of this paper the day after Beltane. Beltane, in my tradition, is a holiday of fertility, renewal, and signifies the height of spring; the epitome of growth and promise. This is quite fitting as I too have experienced an awakening, a type of renaissance of the soul. I have awakened to the fullness of my identity and have been graced with the knowledge and the awareness of my Africana heritage.

This knowledge has been passed down to me and to others through the far reaches of time through oral tradition, spirituality, history, music, dance, and literature. Novels by Africana women are vessels that hold this knowledge. They tell us of our history and our spiritual lineage. The stories that they tell construct a continuity of themes that are echoed through contemporary feminist/womanist literature, anthropology, and spiritual traditions. Through these mediums we are given knowledge of the true nature of the identity of the Africana woman. Through these mediums I invoke the queen.

What is a Queen?

When we think of the Africana woman in America we are not presented with positive images. Our racist, patriarchal culture associates the Africana woman with poverty and carelessness. She is poor and hopelessly tied to the welfare system. She is careless because of the many children that she brings into the world that she cannot feed. She is seen as a weak creature who has failed to thrive. Not only has she failed to thrive, but she continues to bring children into the world who will also fail to thrive. In our American society, the Africana woman is viewed as a helpless nuisance who will continue to add to societal woes by simply reproducing. It is very hard to uncover the truth about the Africana woman when we are presented with these images. However, they are not representative of the true identity of the Africana woman. The true identity of the Africana woman is the queen.

The archetype of the queen is embedded in the psyche of the

Africana woman. It is our birthright. In her article *The African Woman Today* Ama Ata Aidoo states "this is a sorry pass the daughters of the African continent have come to-especially when we remember that they are descended from some of the bravest, most independent, and most innovative women this world has ever known" (Aidoo, 39). She supports this claim with the stories of the Dahomey, who "sought to protect their empire against invaders and internal treachery" (Aidoo, 41). She also speaks of the Asante queen Yaa Asantewa who commandeered battle against the British and is credited with helping to create "the theoretical basis for the political emergence of modern Africa" (Aidoo, 41). Therefore it is plain to see that the blood of beautiful and powerful queens runs through the veins of contemporary Africana women.

The archetype of the African queen is the embodiment of power. An African queen is a powerful mother and warrior who cares for, nurtures, and protects the welfare of the people and has the power to bless as well as curse. If I were to define the word queen with one word, it would be "sovereign:" supreme in power or authority, or having independent authority (Merriam-Webster, 687). The African queen Hatshepsut, an 18th dynasty pharaoh, was the longest reigning female to rule in Egypt and is a living embodiment of the word "sovereign." Even women who are not sole rulers of nations may hold the status of sovereign queenship. For example Priestesses may also be considered queens. In her article *Reconsidering the Mammy Water Myths* Sabine Jell-Bahlsen states that Eze Mmiri, the priestess of Mammy Water is often called "Eze Nwanyi" which means queen. She points out that this title is also bestowed upon the town's oldest woman who is responsible for settling disputes among women" (Jell Bahlsen, 116). It may also be worth noting that the job of the highest ranking male priest of Mammy Water is to 'assist' the priestess" (Jell Bahlsen, 116).

The queen is not just a part of Africana culture. She exists within our American society in many forms. She can be found in pioneering African American women such as Zora Neale Hurston, and in the contemporary singer "India Arie" who names herself queen in her song "Video." She can be found in the music of the self named rap singer "Queen" Latifah who "challenges white patriarchal male power and outlines the ways in which it targets poor black women" (Ransby and Matthews, 532). Modern day queens can be found every time you look into the eyes of an Africana woman who engages in resistance, promotes leadership, and is concerned for the welfare of her community.

The African queen is endowed with beauty, strength, and nurturance. There are Priestess Queens, Warrior Queens, and Queen Mothers. Three of the female pantheon of Yoruba deities embody these characteristics. Oshun, the Yoruba deity of rivers, love, sensuality, and beauty, is considered to be the most attractive of the orisha. Oya, queen of the warrior women and keeper of wisdom is a powerful force to be reckoned with. Yemaya, the mother of the orisha exemplifies all of these characteristics. She is lover, mother, warrior, and witch. The Yoruba Goddesses Oshun, Oya, and Yemaya all embody characteristics of the African Queen. Therefore, they are the orisha that I will invoke in the novels.

Who Is Oshun?

The translation of the word Oshun or Osun means source. It is related to the word_orisun, "the source of a river, people, or of children" (Murphy, 2). For her worshippers Oshun is the ultimate representation of the feminine principle and the queen of the African Diaspora. Her shrine is located in Oshogbo Nigeria, where the Oshun River is located. Oshun has many sexual partners and her love affairs are sacred. Oshun is a virgin in the pagan sense, namely a woman who loves whom she pleases, whenever she pleases, and whose sexuality is sacred (Carnival, 80). Oshun is everything that is beautiful in the world and is associated with honey and bees. She generously feeds the hungry, and her waters bring healing. However, do not underestimate Oshun; she paints her cheeks with the blood of her enemies (Jambalaya, 122). Oshun is the archetype of the African Queen: beautiful, sensual, and fierce. Oshun is of particular interest in female centered African American novels because "Under conditions of enslavement and cultural marginalization, Osun traditions became a key feature of African-Atlantic strategies of adaptation and resistance to European values and spirituality" (Murphy, 4-5). Although Oshun is desired by men, she is a woman-centered Goddess. Only women are allowed in her temple in Oshogbo Nigeria.

Representations of Oshun in Their Eyes Were Watching God

Janie, the central character in the book is a daughter of Oshun. First of all she is beautiful. Her long silken hair and beautiful skin are spoken of many times in the novel. Janie also believes in marriage for love. Her grandmother advises her to marry as soon as possible because she realized that Janie had become a woman. Although Janie insists differently it was obvious that at sixteen Janie was on her way to maturity. This theme is hinted at by the language of the book. "The rose of the world was breathing out smell. It followed her through all her waking moments and caressed her in her sleep" (Hurston, 10).

The understanding of passion comes to Janie through nature. "She saw a dust-bearing bee sink into the sanctum of a bloom; the thousand sister calyxes arch to meet the love embrace and the ecstatic shiver of the tree from root to tiniest branch creaming in every blossom and frothing with delight. So this was marriage! She had been summoned to behold a revelation. Then Janie felt a pain remorseless and sweet that left her limp and languid" (Hurston, 11). After this "revelation" Janie sees Johnny Taylor walking up the road and kisses him. When Nanny sees this she insists that Janie marry Logan Killicks who has been asking for her hand in marriage. Logan has a lot of land and the money to go with it. He represents the security that Nanny wants Janie to have.

Janie marries Logan as her Nanny asks but does not love him. One day she goes to see Nanny and tells of her distress. Janie believes that marriage means love and feels guilty about her inability to love Logan. Nanny tells her that love causes the black woman to suffer and that security is better. Eventually Janie realizes that marriage does not equal love and resigns herself to her situation. However, when Joe Starks comes along Janie realizes that she has not given up on love. She leaves her husband and marries Joe in hopes of a loving partnership. Unfortunately, it does not take Janie long to discover that Joe is not in love with Janie, only the idea of her.

After Joe dies Janie is very happy to be alone. She confided to her friend Phoebe Watson that she loved her freedom and that her mourning for Jo shouldn't last longer than her grief, which is over. It is not until Janie found this inner peace that love came knocking on her door. Love comes in the form of a man named "Tea Cake" who is about twelve years her junior. Janie fought her feelings for him but could not deny what was growing between them. She finally gave into her feelings for Tea Cake, and through her love for him "her soul crawls out of its hiding place." Janie's belief in the power and beauty of love and her pursuit of love in spite of her hardships invokes Oshun, the Yoruba Goddess of love, beauty, and pleasure.

Representations of Oshun in So Long A Letter

The strongest representation of Oshun in So Long a Letter was Ramatoulaye's undying devotion to her husband Modou Fall. She was strongly committed to him and to their love from the very beginning. Her mother advises her to marry Daouda Dieng because he is a successful doctor and showers her mother with gifts. He also is very taken with Ramatoulaye and her mother tells her that "a woman must marry the man who loves her but never the one she loves; that is the secret of lasting happiness" (Ba, 59). Furthermore, her mother does not trust Modou. She found Modou to be "too handsome, too polished, and too perfect" (Ba, 14). Her distrust of him is heightened by his features. She did not trust the wide gap between his two incisors, "the sign of primacy of sensuality in an individual" (Ba, 14)." However, Ramatoulaye defied her mother's wishes and married for love, rather than security.

Ramatoulaye's undying devotion to Modou remained even after her betrayed her. Modou not only chose to remarry, but also created a new and separate life with his daughter's college friend. Modou did not tell her of his indiscretions. Ramatoulaye was informed of his wedding by his brothers after it had already taken place. He never came to see her or his children again, and spent their joint fortune on the maintenance of his new wife and his new mother in law. Although Ramatoulaye was heartbroken and angry with Modou, she could not bring herself to divorce him.

Ramatoulaye showed her love for him yet again after his death when she was asked by two other suitors for her hand in marriage. The second suitor is Daouda Dieng, the suitor she refused so many years ago. Ramatoulaye values his company but cannot bring herself to marry him because she felt only friendship for him.

Ramatoulaye states "I do not love Daouda Dieng. My mind appreciates the man. But heart and mind often disagree" (Ba, 66). She could not face him in public, so she refused his proposal in a letter. She asserts her position by stating "My conscience is not accommodating enough for me to marry you, when only esteem, justified by your many qualities, pulls me toward you. Esteem is not enough for marriage, whose snares I know from experience" (68). Ramatoulaye then asks Daouda for his friendship. However, he is a proud man, and never spoke to her again. Although she was saddened by his rejection she did not yield in her decision. She would rather be alone than to marry a man she did not love. The only man she ever loved is Modou.

The idea of marrying for love is quite foreign in some communitarian African societies. In these societies you are not your own person, you are the property of your family. All that you do in life is connected to the goal of sustaining or bettering your family. Therefore, marriage is seen as a way to bring wealth and honor to the family. Most marriages are arranged for this purpose. To marry for love outside of your parent's wishes is an act of great resistance. This resistance in the name of love invokes the Goddess Oshun.

Who Is Oya?

Oya is the mistress of change and the bringer of wisdom. Oya is a warrior and the changes she brings about are harsh. "Oya does not just rearrange the furniture in the house-she knocks the building to the ground" (Jambalaya, 120). Oya is the wind of the cyclone that destroys in order to create. Oya is the mother of catastrophe: sudden structural change. When women resist cultural norms, and fight against the status quo, they invoke Oya. She is the death bringer and the life giver because every end is a beginning. Woman as warrior is a theme that resonates through history as women resist all forms of oppression. Oya gives women the agency to create change. Oya is the ultimate warrior queen and embodies an aspect of the *Ache*, or the personal power (Jambalaya, 63) of the Africana woman.

Representations of Oya in Their Eyes Were Watching God

Janie invokes the spirit of Oya many times in the novel. Oya in her warrior aspect can be seen in the agency that Janie gives herself in her relationships. Although Janie was forced to marry her first husband and beaten by the next two, she maintains her strong will throughout each relationship.

Janie was unhappy in her first marriage but resigned herself to her situation. However, when she met Joe Starks she left her first husband Logan and married Joe. When Janie left Logan she left behind security and the expectations that had been placed upon her by society. When Joe began to mistreat her she was devastated that he was not the man that she believed him to be. However, on several occasions Janie spoke out against her husband and disregards the strife that it added to their marriage.

Janie shamed him in front of the other men at the store by saying that when he pulls down his britches he looks like "de change uh life" (Hurston, 79). She also criticized him in his last days by telling him that it will take death for him to understand that he has to pacify someone besides himself if he wants any love and sympathy in the world (Hurston, 87). Joe takes his last breath while Janie rebukes him one last time by saying "All dis bowin down, all dis disobedience under yo' voice-dat ain't whut Ah rushed off down de road tuh find out about you" (Hurston, 87). Joe Starks dies with his fists in the air in silent protest.

Janie also shows her warrior spirit when she runs off with Tea Cake. Janie has just lost her husband and Tea Cake is twelve years her junior. Janie leaves her town and everything that she knows to be with him. She is accustomed to luxury but is glad to work by Tea Cake's side in the fields. After the hurricane Tea Cake becomes deranged by rabies and tries to kill Janie. However, she shoots first and kills the man she loves. After Tea cake's death is ruled "accidental;" Janie goes back to the home that she once shared with her previous husband Joe Starks with her head held high.

There are many ways to be a warrior. Contrary to the belief that "uh white man and uh nigger woman is de freest thing on earth" (Hurston, 189) Black women are said to occupy the lowest rung of society. "De white man throw down de load and tell de nigger man tuh pick it up. He pick it up because he have to, but he don't tote it. He hand it to his womenfolks. De nigger woman is de mule uh de world" (Hurston, 14). For a woman to resist in any way in this culture, be it large or small invokes the warrior queen Oya.

Representations of Oya in So Long A Letter

Oya, goddess of wisdom is also invoked by Ramatoulaye. She is an educated woman in a culture where most women are not. She insists that her children be educated as well. Although she is very traditional she desires rights for women and speaks of it many times in the book. She declares that housewives deserve praise for all the work they do (Ba, 63) and how women should have the right to vote and equal paid employment (Ba, 61). I believe that Ramatoulaye is what Luisah Teish would call an "armchair feminist," a woman who embodies the views of feminism but does not speak of it (Jambalaya, 14).

Oya is also invoked through the actions of Ramatoulaye's friend Jacqueline the Ivorian. Jacqueline was a protestant and disobeyed her parents by marrying a Muslim man. However, after she and her husband were married she refused to convert to Islam. Although her in-laws looked down on her, she attended the

Protestant church of her choice every Sunday. Marrying outside of one's religion is a huge taboo in many cultures. However, for a woman in Africa to do this, when she is often considered to be the property of her family is almost unheard of. Similarly in many areas, it is also unheard of for a woman to marry and persist in practicing a different religion different from her husband. This was a great act of resistance and Oya is invoked in her aspect as warrior.

The strongest representation of Oya is embodied through Ramatoulaye's friend Aissatou. She embodies Oya's warrior strength in her determination to marry a man who is far beyond her class. Aissatou, the daughter of a goldsmith marries Mawdo Ba, the son of Seynabou; a princess. Mawdo's mother is angered by this and concocts a plan to take revenge on Aissatou, who she believes has stolen her "only man" from her (Ba, 26). Mawdo's mother fosters her brother's daughter Nabou, puts her into midwifery school and eventually presents her as a second wife for Mawdo. Mawdo cannot refuse this offer because of the shame it would bring upon his mother. He accepts, and Aissatou is the last one to know. Although she is Mawdo's first wife, she and her sons are forgotten.

Aissatou is advised to stay with Mawdo. "You do not burn the tree that bears the fruit...boys cannot succeed without their father (Ba, 31)." However, Aissatou defies tradition. She took her four sons and left Mawdo. Aissatou denounces him in a letter by saying "I am stripping myself of your love, your name. Clothed in my dignity, the only worthy garment, I go my way (Ba, 32)." Although leaving Mawdo was hard for Aissatou, she pours her passion into her books. She was accepted into the School of Interpreters in France and upon graduation accepts an appointment in the Senegalese Embassy in the United States.

Aissatou is the embodiment of Oya. She embodies Oya as warrior by defying tradition. She also embodies Oya's aspect as the Orisha of wisdom through her academic success. However, Aissatou's biggest defiance is her ultimate success as a single educated woman. Her unexpected success is the biggest resistance of all and invokes the spirit of Oya as the queen of the warrior women.

Who is Yemaya

Yemaya is the nurturance that supports all life. She is the deep mysterious ocean and the origin of life. She is the black mermaid who resides within the deep waters, and the deep mysterious moon.

She is the waves that crash against the shore "the constantly coming woman" (Jambalaya, 119). Yemaya is the mother of dreams and the keeper of wisdom so primal and deep that it cannot be understood by human consciousness (Jambalaya, 118). When the slaves were brought to America from Africa, they prayed to Yemaya for protection.

Yemaya as mother of all life is a very powerful symbol for many Africana women. In Africa motherhood is considered a woman's most sacred duty. The children of the Africana woman are her "wealth" and her "ticket to immortality" (Jambalaya, 73). As all good mothers, the love of Yemaya is both benevolent and harsh. Yemaya's wish to nurture and provide may prove deadly. If you grieve too long, she may take you into her murky depths in order to provide comfort. During the middle passage some of the slaves jumped overboard so that they could be received by the salty womb of the mother.

Representations of Yemaya in Their Eyes Were Watching God

Yemaya is invoked in the book several times by Nanny, Janie's grandmother. Glimpses of Yemaya are first seen in Nanny through the description of Janie's childhood. Janie and Nanny lived on the property of a white couple and their family. Janie did not realize that she was different from the other children until she saw her reflection in a picture and realized that she was colored. As Janie grew older she was teased by other black children for living on property which belonged to white people. Janie's grandmother felt badly about this and moved them off the land. This was hard for Nanny as she had the help and camaraderie of Mrs. Watson, the white mistress of the house. She moved away from this comfort out of her love for Janie.

Nanny showed a harsher aspect of the mother when she insisted that Janie marry Logan Killicks. She knew that Logan was many years Janie's senior and that she did not want to marry him. However, she was concerned for Janie's welfare. She saw her kissing Johnny Taylor and insists that she "don't want no trashy nigger, no breath-and britches, lak Johnny Taylor usin' yo' body to wipe his foots on" (Hurston, 13). She suffered when she saw her daughter, Leafy, running around with different men. Nanny didn't want the same fate for Janie. Logan Killicks was a good man with ten acres of land and Janie would be well taken care of. She insists "Taint Logan Killicks Ah wants you to have, baby, it's protection"

(Hurston, 15).

During the course of their conversation, Nanny reveals her Leafy's legacy. Nanny was a young woman during the days of slavery and was raped repeatedly by the owner of the plantation. This is how Janie's mother Leafy came into the world. The Mistress of the plantation knew what was going on and asked to see Nanny's baby. She knew by looking that Leafy was her husband's child. She beat Nanny and told her that the next day the overseer would give Nanny one hundred lashes for what she'd done. She stated coldly "Ah'll have you whipped till de blood run down to yo' heels!....And if it kills you Ah'll stand de loss. Anyhow, as soon as dat brat is a month old Ah'm going to sell it offa dis place" (Hurston, 18)."

Nanny was not yet healed from Leafy's birth. However she took both of their lives into her hands and ran away from the plantation. She hid in the swamp by the river and breast fed her baby every time she cried so they would not be discovered. Nanny hid there until she heard that the end of the war was near, and then rejoined other black people with others. When the war was over she went to live with the Washburns who Janie grew up with. She never married because she did not want anyone to mistreat her baby, the bastard child of a slave master.

Nanny worked very hard to "make de sun shine on both sides of de street" (Hurston, 19) for Janie's mother. She even put her in school to become a teacher someday. However all her dreams were crushed when the schoolteacher raped Leafy at the age of seventeen and became pregnant with Janie. Leafy never recovered from the trauma of the rape and drowns her pain in men and alcohol. Eventually she runs off and leaves Janie with Nanny. Nanny had hoped that Janie would become a schoolteacher. However, when she sees Janie's growing passion her protection instincts kick in. The only way that Nanny could insure Janie's protection is by Janie's marriage to Logan Killicks. Nanny hates to push Janie into a loveless marriage to an older man. However, her insistence comes from a maternal instinct to protect her child. Nanny embodies Yemaya, the mother of all life through her brave struggle to attend to the welfare of her daughter and her granddaughter.

Representations of Yemaya in So Long a Letter

Although both Oshun and Oya are represented in *So Long a Letter*, it is Yemaya who stands out most. Even though Ramatoulaye is

Muslim she also embodies qualities and characteristics of a daughter of Yemaya. Yemaya as the great mother is referred to many times in the book by the actions of Ramatoulaye, and also her school teacher who desired an "uncommon destiny" for her students (Ba, 15). Ramatoulaye reminisces fondly of her school days and remembers that her teacher loved her students without patronizing them and knew how to appreciate their qualities (Ba, 16).

This same philosophy was passed down to Ramatoulaye who sees her job as a teacher as a "priesthood." She states that in her students she and the other teachers "set in motion waves that breaking, carried away in their furl a bit of ourselves" (Ba, 23). It is also interesting that she refers to the children as "waves" as Yemaya is the ruler of the ocean. Ramatoulaye is metaphorically saying that the students are the children of Yemaya, and she is a priestess of Yemaya, who approaches her task with love and understanding, just as her teacher did.

Ramatoulaye is a wonderful mother. Her children are her source of joy when she is left by her husband. She takes pride in them and believes that the success of the nation depends on the success of the family (Ba, 89). However, Ramatoulaye's most poignant portrayal of Yemaya occurred when she discovered out that her eldest daughter was pregnant. Having an unmarried pregnant daughter in Senegalese Muslim society is perhaps the greatest shame that can be brought upon a mother. At first Ramatoulaye is furious at her daughter and her lack of regret over the affair that led to her pregnancy.

However, Ramatoulayes's anger eventually melts and she realizes that the child inside her daughter is "demanding protection." She comforts her daughter and realizes that "one is a mother to understand the inexplicable. One is a mother to lighten the darkness. One is a mother to shield when lightening streaks the night, when thunder shakes the earth, when mud bogs one down. One is a mother to love without beginning or end" (Ba, 82-83).

After learning of her oldest daughters pregnancy, Ramatoulaye has "the talk" with her other daughters and gives them contraceptives. Although it pains her very much to do this, Ramatoulaye states that "modern mothers... remove any thorn or pebble that might hinder the progress of her children towards the conquest of all forms of liberty" (Ba, 87). Ramatoulaye abandoned her traditional values and beliefs for the love of her children. She met with her daughter's boyfriend and realized that a new family is being formed before her eyes. She is saddened, but realizes that "the ripe fruit must drop away from the tree" (Ba, 86). Ramatoulaye enters the rite of passage that all mothers must go through when she chooses to love her daughter enough to let her go. She handles this rite with grace, and with love. Ramatoulaye is Yemaya.

In search of a Lesbian Queen

Oshun, Oya, and Yemaya, whom I call the sacred trio, are repeatedly invoked in *So Long a Letter* and in *Their Eyes Were Watching God*. If I were to read more novels written by Africana women, I am sure that the sacred trio would repeatedly appear. The continuity of themes represented by the sacred trio is inherent in the lived experience of many Africana women. The roles of lover, mother, and warrior are the birthright of the Africana woman. How could I not feel a connection to this culture and to these women? However, this connection is tinged with hurt and bitterness as I recall the many times that I have been rebuked by the African American Community for who and how I love.

Homophobia is extremely prominent in the African American community. I remember the rejection of the black community in college who merely "tolerated" my relationship with another woman because I was a booming voice for minority student affairs and the Vice president of the Coalition for Ethnic Awareness. I have painful memories of arguments and awkward silences. The homophobia that I experienced from people of color hurt because I was being rejected by my allies. Sadly enough, being part of the Coalition for Ethnic Awareness in college was my first experience of black community. It hurt to finally have the community I had always wanted and to still feel like such an outsider.

It is painful to hear that many people discount Oya from the court of the seven African powers because she is "just a dyke." It is even more painful to hear that some have expressed disapproval of Luisah Teish for initiating Lesbians into African spiritual traditions tradition, although my hat is off to her for doing so. It is more painful still to read Olabisi Aiana's statement that issues concerning the rights of gays and lesbians are outside of the agenda of African Feminism because "for many African societies lesbianism and homosexuality are nothing but abominations" (Aina, 73). In the past, this recurring theme deterred me from my exploration into my culture. However, I am now seeking out black lesbian role models who embody the Queen. My search has led me to Cheryl Clarke.

I was delighted to discover Cheryl Clarke's work. The women's studies programs in many schools are not presenting work by black feminists. Even less are presenting work by black lesbian feminists. In fact, the title black lesbian feminist was somewhat of a myth to me. I knew that they existed, but I sure hadn't seen any. Furthermore, the only black feminist that I had even heard of was Belle Hooks. Alice Walker had been mentioned, but only in relation to *The Color Purple*. I would not even have known that Cheryl Clarke existed if it were not for my graduate school teacher Arisika's Razak's insistence on including literature by lesbian women in her curriculum for the Women's spirituality program at the California Institute of Integral Studies. If it were not for Arisika Razak, the term "black lesbian feminism" and the work of Cheryl Clarke would have remained in the mythological realm. Through her work Cheryl Clarke embodies Oshun, Oya, and Yemaya.

Cheryl Clarke and Oshun

Cheryl Clarke embodies Oshun by the work that she does in the world. The work that she has done for the black lesbian feminist community comes from a place of love. Her work as a lesbian is motivated by her physical, spiritual, and emotional love for women. Her work as a feminist is motivated by her universal love for all women. She states "As far as I am concerned, any woman who calls herself a feminist must commit herself to the liberation of *all* women...The lesbian- feminist struggles for the liberation of all people from patriarchal domination" (Clarke, 243). I can identify with what Cheryl is saying on a personal level. I have often said to others that to me, feminism is inherent in lesbianism. As a lesbian, I love women so much that I want to create a world that treats them as the sacred beings that they are. Feminism is the vehicle that I use to do this work. I am dedicated to the Goddess Oshun and just like Cheryl Clarke, both my lesbianism and feminism come from a place of passion and love ; the realm of Oshun.

Cheryl Clarke and Oya

"For a woman to be a lesbian in a male-supremacist, capitalist, misogynist, racist, homophobic, imperialist culture, such as that of North America, is an act of resistance" (Clarke, 242). I could not have said this better myself. Cheryl Clarke is living her truth and demanding her right to love freely in a world where "freedom" is often a myth. She is not only living her truth, but also writing about it. This article was written over two decades ago when the reality of being an "out " lesbian in society was much harsher than it is today. Aside from her work in lesbian feminism, Cheryl Clarke also earned a PhD. Even today, there is an astonishingly low percentage of African American women with doctoral degrees. Cheryl Clarke has not only forged a name for herself in academia, but has also created nontraditional scholarship that challenges cultural norms. This is an amazing feat for any woman. However, as an African American woman it is phenomenal. The warrior spirit of Cheryl Clarke is evident through her life and through her work. Cheryl Clarke is a warrior for women who brings drastic change through wisdom. She is a daughter of Oya.

Cheryl Clarke and Yemaya

In my opinion one of the tasks or goals of a mother is to unify, or bring together. A mother strives for unity in her home because it creates peace. Cheryl Clarke shows her affinity for unity in her desire to eradicate some of the problems in the black lesbian feminist community. She addresses the division between black lesbians who date other black women and black lesbians who date white women. She talks about the fact that she is tired of black lesbians who date white women being demonized and considered "unloyal" to the black lesbian feminist community. She states "We, as black lesbians must vehemently resist being bound by the white man's racist, sexist laws, which have endangered potential intimacy of any kind between whites and blacks" (Clarke, 248).

Cheryl admits that oppression experienced by white women is different than that of black women. However, both have been oppressed by the patriarchal system and "should stop fighting each other for our space at the bottom, because there ain't no more room" (Clarke, 250). Her desire for unity is reinforced in her belief that if lesbians can learn to love each other across racial lines, than that will be the "final resistance" (Clarke, 250). Cheryl Clarke's desire to unify and create peace in her community by fostering racial harmony is a form of nurturance. This nurturance is inspired by Yemaya, the Yoruba mother of all life.

In Search of an Ancestor Queen

I have often felt that I have been cut off from my black ancestry. Growing up with a white mother in an all white town did not lend itself to discussions on black history or culture. My biological mother, a white woman, was the rebel of the family for partnering and having a child with a black man. When my mother died, and I was adopted by her sister, my blackness became a "non issue." I often felt like my family just "pretended" that I wasn't black. I later found out that much of their racism was borne from anger and resentment over my father's treatment of my mother.

I have finally discovered the primacy, beauty and strength of the African woman. I no longer connect my blackness with my father, but with the rich history and spiritual lineage of my African Queen mothers. Ancestor reverence is an integral part of many African spiritual traditions. This element is problematic for me as I no longer have access to my father's family, nor to him. Therefore I have decided to create my own ancestry. I believe that an ancestor does not necessarily have to be a blood relative. So I have chosen a worthy queen as my taken ancestor; Gamba Adisa, Audre Lorde.

Audre Lorde was given the name Gamba Adisa late in life. The name means "Warrior: She who makes her meaning clear" (lanmda.net). Audre Lorde was a self described "black lesbian, mother, warrior poet." She was all the things that I am and hope to be in this life. Audre was Oya in her work as an activist and an educator. She was Oshun in her creative work and her commitment to the erotic. She was Yemaya in her physical role as mother and the unity she strived to create in the black, lesbian, and feminist communities. Audre Lorde was a modern day queen, and I claim her as part of my lineage.

The Queen In Me

Audre Lorde's statement "I have come to believe over and over again that what is most important to me must be spoken, made verbal and shared, even at the risk of having it bruised or misunderstood" (lambda.net) has great meaning to me. I try to live by this principle every day of my life. I try to live and speak my truth in the hope that it will encourage others to live and speak theirs.

I embrace my power as queen. I know that within me there is a lover, a mother, and a warrior. I know that there is a mother, a lover, and a warrior in all women. My work in this life is to help women to remember who they are so that they may stand up and claim the power that is rightfully theirs. I also wish for men to rise up and claim their true identities instead of passively accepting the roles that patriarchal culture has handed them. I wish for every living thing to be held sacred. I wish to be an agent of change.

May Oshun help me to walk with love

May Oya help me to fight for what is right

May Yemaya help me to birth a new world

ACHE!

Bibliography

Aidoo, Ama Ata. "The African Woman Today" Sisterhood, Feminisms, & Power. Trenton, NJ: Africa World Press, 1998

Aina, Olabisi. "African Women at the Grassroots: The Silent Partners of the Women's Movement" Sisterhood, Feminisms, & Power. Trenton, NJ: Africa World Press, 1998

Ba, Mariama. So Long a Letter. Johannesburg, South Africa: Heinemann Publishers Ltd, 1989.

Clarke, Cheryl. "Lesbianism: An Act of Resistance" Words of Fire: an Anthology of African-American Feminist Thought. Ed. Beverly Guy-Sheftall, New York: New Press 2004.

Hurston, Zora Neale. Their Eyes Were Watching God. New York, NY: Harper Perennial Modern Classics, 2006.

Jell-Bahlsen, Sabine. "Eze Mmiri Di Egwu, The Water Monarch is Awesome: Reconsidering the Mammy Water Myths" Ed. Kaplan, Flora Edouwaye Queens, Queen Mothers, Priestesses and Power: Case Studies in African Gender. New York: NY Acad. of Sciences, 1997.

Murphy, Joseph and Mei-Mei Sanford "Introduction." Osun Across the Waters. Eds. Murphy, Joseph and Mei-Mei Sanford. Bloomington: IN UP, 2001.

Ransby, Barbara and Tracy Matthews. "Discourse of Resistance" Words of Fire: an Anthology of African-American Feminist Thought. Ed. Beverly Guy-Sheftall, New York: New Press 2004.

Teish, Luisah. Carnival of the Spirit: Seasonal Celebrations and Rites of Passage. San Francisco CA: Harper San Francisco, 1994.

Teish, Luisah. Jambalaya: The Natural Woman's Book of Personal Charms and Practical Rituals. San Francisco CA: Harper San Francisco, 1985.

Secondary Sources

The Merriam-Webster Dictionary. Springfield MA: Merriam-Webster Incorporated, 2004

REMEMBER...Those Who Kicked Down the Doors/Audre Lorde http://www.lambda.net/~maximum/lorde.html

The Moon in my Mouth

Szmeralda Shanel

One of my favorite novels is Ntozake Shange's *Sassafrass, Cypress, and Indigo*. The story follows the lives of three African American sisters as they grow from girls to women. When the story begins, Shange tells us:

Where there is a woman there is magic. If there is a moon falling from her mouth, she is a woman who knows her magic, who can share or not share her powers. A woman with a moon falling from her mouth, roses between her legs and tiaras of Spanish moss, this woman is a consort of the spirits.

We are then introduced to Indigo, and are told that she has a moon in her mouth. When her mother tries to trim the roses around her thighs and between her legs or pull the moss tiaras on her head, Indigo tells her that it will all just grow back because it's in her blood, that she's got earth blood filled with the Gee-chees long gone and the sea.

Indigo creates dolls from almost anything. They are her companions, and they also keep track of her changes, her moods and her dreams--these dolls talk to her in her sleep. We are told that Indigo and her dolls discuss secret things that have nothing to do with Jesus, and that her mother would simply shake her head.

Indigo had knowledge of the old ways. Her mother worried that the child had too much of the South in her, and that is an example of how many African Americans, in an attempt to seem more educated or sophisticated or to be taken more seriously or to become "good" Christians, abandoned certain ways of being, which they felt were too "country."

A lot of those ways of being had to do with so called superstitions and old wives tales. It meant not talking about the dreams a person had the night before or what root could be used for what purpose. In the United States, it is in the South that our magical-spiritual ancestral traditions have survived the most.

I too was born with a moon in my mouth; the first time I was aware of it falling was when I was about five years old. I woke up one night and saw my older brother sitting in the living room on the couch. I was very excited to see him because I had not seen him in quite some time, but I was also very tired. I decided to go back to sleep and talk with him in the morning.

When I got up the next morning I started running around the house looking for him. When my mother asked me what I was doing, I told her about the night before; the expression on my mother's face told me that something was very wrong. She shook her head and said, "No, you had a dream, and don't say that again." She then turned and walked away from me; she was very upset. My brother had died about a year earlier. I did not mention seeing him to her again (nor did I ever see him or any other physical manifestation of a spirit again). I swallowed the moon and stayed quiet about such things... for a while anyway.

By the time I was in high school I was having precognitive dreams. When I went to my mother about this, she informed me that she "dreamed true" as well. She was not at all interested in exploring these things, they had been happening to her all her life, and she found it all a bit creepy. She also told me that she believed I had seen my brother those many years ago, but at the time she just couldn't go there with me. My mother is from the South and not unfamiliar with the old hoodoo beliefs and magical practices of our ancestors that survived there. Still, she worked hard to dismiss these things as coincidences and superstitions. She may have been able to succeed if I weren't so persistent and curious.

For fun I started reading palms and tarot cards, which my mother gave me for Christmas when I was sixteen, for friends and family. My readings were accurate. At the same time I was becoming increasingly dissatisfied with the Christian church. Like Indigo, the conversations I had with my magical playmates had nothing to do with Jesus. I did recognize and believe in the magic and power in the Christian religion, my grandfather was a preacher and I had witnessed the anointing ceremonies and hands on healing that he and my grandmother did in their church. I also found the teachings of Christ to be beautiful, but the dogma of Christianity, the sexism and the intense focus on sin and redemption were too oppressive for my spirit.

While my mother continued to go to church she told me that she did so because it was the only religion that she really knew, that no one group of people had the right way to God and that it was okay for me to find God for myself wherever that may be. Eventually my work with the Tarot led me to the Goddess. But there was still something wrong. All of the information I was finding was on Wicca, and while it seemed close to what I was looking for, I was not Wiccan. I could visit Wiccan circles, and they were okay, but I knew that this was not my home. I read Luisah Teish's book *Jambalaya* and started learning about Ifa and the Orisha and this excited me, but I was in Chicago and Teish was in Oakland, so I continued to read and pray and listen.

The Dark Mother

Isis started to come to me in dreams. I would have these vivid vibrant dreams of Isis from which I would wake feeling this ecstasy and longing that felt like... I don't know, nothing I'd ever felt before. This really had me confused because in my waking life I was not particularly drawn to Isis but as many of her devotees have said, Isis calls her clergy and it was the same with me. I must admit at first I was a little resistant. I thought I knew who she was, and I was not interested in a soft sacrificing mother Goddess of love and light. I was/am an Amazon, I needed a warrior queen. Once I stopped being arrogant, surrendered and answered the call, she revealed herself to me as Black Isis, she told me,

I am Isis the Nubian. Auset.
The Great Cosmic Star Goddess. Mother of all.
Black Virgin I belong to myself. Magician. Trickster. I gave birth to myself.
I am the beginning and the end. The nurturer and the destroyer.
I am the Silent Serpent, my stinging venom the poison and the antidote.
Veiled. I see all.
I am the sacred whore. My honey coated thighs intoxicating, sweet, dangerous.
I am rapture, I am chaos. Surrender.
True freedom is found in me, the Dark Mother Black Isis.

Most of what I know of Black Isis/Auset/the Dark Mother are mysteries that have unfolded for me and are difficult to express in a linear way. My experiences are poetic, they come from trance/journey and flow like dreams--sometimes I start at the end then move from there to the beginning and from there I end in the middle. I come out knowing something on a deep intuitive level; I then do research to see if I can find anything to support my new discoveries. I believe the divine African Dark Mother Isis/Auset is goddess of 10,000 names because she is all Goddesses and she is mother of all Gods and Goddesses. All Goddesses are daughters of the Dark Mother and they are all faces and expressions of the Dark Mother. When I speak of Black Isis I do not mean the daughter of Nuit or the wife of Osiris, I'm speaking of the Goddess she was before the Egyptians adopted her. I am speaking of the most ancient one, the primordial Goddess, the self-created virgin (meaning unwed/independent) Goddess who contains all (including the male) within.

The African origins of modern humans have been confirmed by archaeologists, geneticists and paleontologists. DNA research demonstrates that modern humans (Homo sapiens) appear to have first emerged 100,000 years ago in east and south Africa. After 50,000 BCE, these Africans walked or sailed to all continents of the world. When Africans began to migrate from sub-Saharan Africa, they took with them to each new continent the religion and art of the Dark mother, Black Isis of Africa (Birnbaum, 2001).

Images of the horned Goddess that would later be known as Auset/Hathor have been found in caves on the presently inaccessible plateau in the center of what is now the Sahara desert. Sub-Saharan Africa, the place where humans emerged is the richest in pre-historic rock art of any place in the world. The rock paintings found in central and south Africa have a predominance of the color red or purple and are characterized by spirals, straight or wavy lines, petals, and concentric circles in series. These are all symbols of the woman divinity of prehistory. Figurines of full-bellied women with large breasts and buttocks called "Venuses" have been found along African migration paths into Europe--from Sicily to Italy to France, Austria, the former Czechoslovakia, Germany, Bulgaria and Romania. The hair on the Venus of Willendorf in Austria is arranged in cornrows, an African style that Sistas are still rockin today. These ancient artistic representations of the Dark Mother of Africa have nearly identical characteristics and have been found all over the world. Science has confirmed the oldest mother we know as African Black and female, science and art confirm the oldest divinity we know as African Black and female (Birnbaum, 2001).

A Religion of Art

The arts originate in the spiritual practice of Shamanism. You look at the earth and you know the Goddess is the greatest artist. In all of nature you find rhythm and music and movement and color and texture and poetry. For me art is a spiritual practice, I am an artist, witch, priestess, and not in that order. As a priestess of sacred arts I am deeply committed to the magical potential of the arts and more specifically to the artistic process to heal, empower and transform an individual as well as an entire community. The arts are not merely forms of entertainment, objects or commodities, they are magical forces and tools of transformation.

In her book, *The White Wand* (2003), Feri witch and priestess Anaar says, "For practitioners of sacred art, art is a verb--an active principle, it demands an act of doing." She goes on to say that through the Shamanic process of art making we receive spiritual revelation from our highest selves, and I would add, the ancestors, the Goddess and other spirits. She also reminds us that all of the arts are of the same source--the Goddess, that while there may be three phases of the moon, there is only one moon. Sacred art is devotional, it is a prayer, a magical act, a way to connect, understand, release and transform. All of our ancestors held this wisdom; it is made known to us through cave paintings, traditional rituals/ceremonies including costuming, folk songs and dances, Goddess figures and teaching stories. For them, there was no boundary between art and spirituality, for indigenous people of today the same is true.

I joined the Fellowship of Isis in 2001, became an ordained priestess of Isis in 2006 and founded the Iseum of Black Isis, a mystery school dedicated to sacred arts and Goddess spirituality in 2007. I have studied with teachers of various spiritual traditions, Isis is still my greatest teacher and hers is the tradition of my heart. She has taken me to sweat lodges, Bembes (Orisha rituals), Pujas (Indian ceremonies), Pagan circles, Buddhist temples; I listen, she leads. For real, she even had me sitting up in church a couple times this year. She has taken great care with my spiritual training. My personal practice is ecstatic/shamanic, and while I am dedicated to Isis, I work with and have deep relationships with my ancestors, various Gods, Goddesses and spirit teachers. Ritual, song, rhythm, dance, story, poetry and color, all shape the core of my spiritual practices, like the ancestors, mine is a religion of art.

Africa

I am a Black American; I do not romanticize Africa or pretend to be African or claim spiritual traditions of Africa that I have not been initiated into or that have not been a part of my culture as a Black American. Still, I trace all of my spiritual beliefs/inheritances/ traditions back to Africa. First as a priestess of the dark mother

Isis/Auset (though there are plenty of white pagans who say as an Egyptian Goddess Isis is not African), and guess what y'all? Egypt is not located on the continent of Africa....right. I've seen enough white artistic representations of mama Yemaya, to feel certain that at some point in the future folks will be trying to say she isn't black or African either...

I also trace my spiritual tradition back to Africa as an initiate in the Anderson Feri tradition. Victor Anderson said, or I should say wrote because I never spoke with him, that the Feri tradition came out of Africa. He also says he was initiated in 1926 by a priestess from Africa. I've been told by one of Victor's students and initiates that in at least one line of Feri there is evidence of this priestess. Still I hear others in the Feri community say that Feri has mysterious roots and no one really knows where it came from. And in regards to Victor being initiated by a priestess from Africa, "Well, Victor said a lot of things." To which my response is "Yes, he did, and how do you decide which things to repeat and which things to dismiss?"

Finally, I practice Hoodoo, which is African American folk magic. When Africans were enslaved and brought to the Americas our spiritual beliefs and practices took different forms. In Brazil, the Dominican Republic and Cuba, the tradition held strongest as Candomble, Shango and Santeria, while in Haiti and Louisiana it was in the form of Vodoun. Hoodoo was established during slavery in the other southern states of the U.S. (Bird, 2004). This African-based magical/spiritual tradition used the available plants in the United States and integrated the wisdom of Native Americans. Hoodoo is not a religion, it is an American magical tradition with roots in Africa that is practiced by people of various religions. The primary concerns of hoodoos are blessings of the home, gaining a partner, good health, luck, happiness, divination, hexing or controlling another person, finding a job, etc. The practice includes rituals, charms/mojos, herbs, stones, sticks and spells. (Bird, 2004).

I have noticed that many White Pagans avoid calling Hoodoo African American folk magic when asked to define it. They like to say things like "Well, Hoodoo is a mixture of things, it has influences from Europe as well as Native America." I'd like to remind folks that African American is not an exclusive term. Black culture is a Creole culture. Anything that's African American will have influences from other cultures given the fact that African Americans are multi-racial people of African descent born and living in America. I have European and Native American ancestry and guess what folks--I'm Black. The African derived magical/spiritual tradition of Hoodoo has influences from Europe and Native America because when my ancestors were enslaved, stolen from their land and brought to this land, they had to work with what was available to them. Hoodoo attests to their creativity and adaptability.

Jazz, the Blues and Hip Hop are African American styles of music that speak to the joy, pain, struggle, survival and strength that are central and specific to Black American culture. These musical art forms allow us to creatively express, endure and examine our experiences as a people in this country. The magical/spiritual tradition of Hoodoo aided and ensured the physical and spiritual survival of Black people during slavery and Jim Crow and continues to support many of us while living in a land where the system of racism that enslaved our ancestors is still strongly intact.

I find it interesting that Cat Yronwode, the teacher that most Pagan folks today are learning Hoodoo from, has been very clear in stating that Hoodoo is African American folk magic, and that she herself learned from Black people. I don't know why her students have such a hard time acknowledging the same. I am not saying that White Pagans should not practice Hoodoo; I am saying when you avoid calling Hoodoo what it is you are being disrespectful to the ancestors and the culture of African Americans. So yeah, obviously there are some problems I see in the Pagan community as it stands today.

Sista. Priestess. Witch

I have also been pleasantly surprised by folks in the Pagan community. The Iseum of Black Isis led a ritual at the Pantheacon 2010 convention called *Conjurers, Root Women, Vodou Queens and Hoodoo Mamas*. It was a ritual in honor of women healers of Africa and the Diaspora. It was our first time leading a ceremony at Pantheacon and nearly one hundred women showed up. The women were of various backgrounds but the majority of them were white. I was surprised that so many women, white women showed up to honor the women healers of my ancestral spiritual traditions. And they didn't just physically show up, they showed up with all of their hearts, souls and spirits. In one part of the ceremony we all sang together in praise of the Dark mother "Mother of all, Dark mother, first mother, the mother of us all. Mother of all, Black mother, first mother, the mother of us all. Hear us oh mother your daughters sing for you, mother of all." To look around the room and see women remembering where we all came from and how and why we are all connected was the real magic. Ashe.

In planning for this ritual with my sista priestesses (black women I've met on the path who also have moons falling from their mouths), we discussed how we would feel or what might happen if a sista showed up to the ceremony who was an initiate in one of the African traditional religions, would she respect us or just think we were playing around? Would she wonder why we had chosen to do things this way rather than the old school traditional way? And did we care? This is something that comes up for many Black folks in the Pagan community, why wouldn't we just go train and initiate into the traditions of Ifa, Vodoun, Mami Wata or Akan? These traditions have never lost the Goddess, there are unbroken lines of practice and if you have ever been to a ceremony in one of these traditions you know it--the magic is strong, the spirits come quickly, the energy is constantly moving, it is the real deal.

As the voice for the sistas who sat in circle with me the day this subject came up, I will say, while we have love and respect for the African traditional religions of our ancestors and we are all dedicated to and work with the Orisha, the Loa, the Mami Watas of west Africa, these traditions have a hierarchical structure and orthodox beliefs that many of us who are seeking spiritual autonomy and empowerment just can't fit in or adhere to, at least not at the time that I'm writing this. We ended the conversation on the final note that we didn't care who showed up, we were doing the work of the Goddess and honoring our ancestors and couldn't nobody have nothin to say about that. That's what we said, but when it actually came time for the ceremony and Chief Iyanifa Lusiah Teish and Iya Oshogbo, two highly respected Ifa elders and priestesses in the community walked in the room, I can't lie, I had an "Oh, shit... we better not fuck this up" moment. It passed and things went beautifully. At the end of the ceremony Oshogbo said to me "It is so nice to see you young ladies continuing to do the work we've been doing for so long." She and Teish stayed after for a while to chat and laugh with us. We all felt so honored to have the support, respect and encouragement of our elders.

All praises to the Black women elders in our spiritual communities. These wise mothers of spirit have illuminated the path that the Goddess has led many of us to. As priestesses, oracles, teachers, healers and leaders they have given us so much, and I am grateful. May we daughters doing the work of spirit be equally honorable examples of how to walk the path in grace, strength, power and beauty for the sistas that come after us. Ashe.

References

Bird, S. R. *Sticks, Stones, Roots & Bones: Hoodoo, Mojo & Conjuring with Herbs.* St. Paul, MN: Llewellyn, 2004

Birnbaum, L.C. *Dark mother: African Origins and Godmothers.* New York: University Press, 2001

Niino, April (Anaar). *The White Wand: Ruminations, Meditations, Reflections toward a Feri Aesthetic.* (self published?), 2003

Shange, N. *Sassafrass, Cypress & Indigo: a Novel.* New York: San Martin's Press, 1982

I Understand It...

Crystal Blanton

There is always a difference; sometimes subtle and sometimes not. Like many of my culture, I was raised to see and acknowledge the differences in who I was as a black woman in society. I was raised around many non-blacks and always been quite comfortable with that but it did not mean that I was not conditioned to understand my history and how that relates to the way the world might view me in it. I never looked at it as a fault or a negative thing; I just have known inherently that I was different, I was a black woman.

I never truly understood the impact of this until I was leaving elementary school to go into middle school and was told I could no longer be friends with my best friend at the time. She was Asian and although her parents were great to me, they were afraid of how their daughter would be perceived as she got older and was friends with a little black girl. I was told I could not be her friend anymore, "people would not understand". This was one of the first times I encountered what it might mean to others that I was not just a girl but a black girl. As shocking as it was for me to hear this and to deal with the heartache; I was trained to know that this might happen someday. The knowing didn't take away the pain but it helped to shape how I saw myself and the experiences I might have.

Since that crucial time in my youth other things have happened, some were small and others were not. I was no longer shocked when the man at the gas station would not touch my hand or my brother's hand while we were exchanging money, although he did for the person before and behind us. Those two people were different from us, they were not black. No matter how much I wanted to dismiss it as a weird occurrence, I knew why and it hurt. I was 14 years old.

I wasn't surprised at the time when my son ran home crying because some kids stole his bike and called him a Nigger. I knew why and it hurt. He was 14 years old.

These events did not color hate against people who were white, they were just a part of life growing up black and existing among others who may not like me before even knowing me. I am sure you can imagine what it is then like to open to others spiritually, in hopes that they do understand or that they will not guess at my character based on the shade of my skin. I have been lucky, most have not.

Sometimes the differences have been so subtle that I have had to explain to coveners how it feels to be of color in certain situations or why some things hurt when it has a different effect on them. I have a pair of colored lenses that I wear through my life; I am a black woman and generations of experiences flow through my blood and my psyche. I tried to explain to two coven sisters why I wanted to cry when we were eating ice cream and a car of white teenagers pulled up and told me that "Oakland was *that* way". As if I were lost, as if I was in the wrong part of town. Once again I knew why and it hurt.

As an adult, I understand so much more about my experiences of race and how that has helped to shape who I am as a spiritual being. In the fundamentalist theory of sociology it is believed that society is created by systematic structures and the failure of such structures create social problems. The system has never really worked for the black person in America and this has continued to create social inequities that have defined the shaping events that contribute to the psychology of black people. I have never known slavery in my lifetime, thank the Gods, but that does not mean that the lingering effects of such severe oppression have not effected who I have become and how I see the world. The conditioning of black people is based on years of oppression that have been passed down by generation, by society and through collective energetic lines of energy from our ancestors.

I do not walk through my life afraid of being black or scared to be a part of any community that is not black. I take great pride in who I am, who I have become and who I will continue to grow into. I have always been able to walk into the Pagan community with a sense of purpose, even if fear of not being accepted mingled with my pride. I have found great acceptance in the Pagan community and due to the path of Paganism I follow, Wicca, I spend a lot of worship time with those who are not minorities. I don't feel judged but I always know that I see through different lenses and have different understandings of life; I am a black woman.

I don't have to reinforce to the coven members or community members that my skin is different or what that means, the spiritual world is one place I do not believe has a spot for that. I approach my spiritual life valuing the differences I have and believing that I will find respect and acceptance for just that. I love those I circle with for not making my differences a hindrance to our relationship when we connect with the God and Goddess; although I might understand it, it would hurt.

I know that being a Bay Area native allows me more flexibility and freedom in being who I am and defining that for other people. I am lucky to be able to be Black and a Wiccan without much fear of the views of others. I know I am lucky and that others are not as lucky as I. I take this as a sign that I can further the mission of grand support and acceptance within the spiritual path of Paganism; I don't have to fight. I get to enjoy the love of my community and the Gods while adding a little color to the canvas, this is a blessing. My face supports the notion that we have the chance to live a life of spirituality within Paganism and support the progression of acceptance for all races, creeds, ethnicities and sexes. I have been blessed with having a gift that makes me a little different. I am blessed with being a black woman.

While there is no such thing as a color blind society, I choose to live in a world where the color of my skin connects to great importance for my life, my children and my community. Being black will always bring concerns that I cannot avoid and I will always get upset at the ignorance of racism but I live a life rich in history and survival that gives me the power to overcome. I have to teach my children what it means to be a black person in America, just as I was taught, but I also surround them with the rainbow of races and support a life rich in personal acceptance regardless of the inequalities in a time of systematic racism that continues to flourish despite huge steps forward within society.

I know that my hand is the darkest one in the ritual circle but it is just as capable to call in the Goddess with as any other. I understand and that does not hurt.

I know that I may have to remind my covenmates why I cannot go into the pool and have "wash and wear" hair for tomorrow. I know we will all laugh at the image of my afro while I sit in a swimsuit. I am not ashamed, I understand it and I am not hurt.

I know that the election of the first Black president will have a different meaning to me than some others and that not everyone's mother cried tears of joy at the image of something she never thought she would see in her lifetime. My mother died weeks after President Obama's inauguration. I understood her tears and I was proud.

I am a walking manifestation of the ability to be who we are and be with those we have chosen to be with, regardless of race. As the Gods have chosen our lessons for us, so we are to acknowledge that as we learn the lesson, we are the lesson. As I gain acceptance within Wicca, so I learn to accept myself and teach acceptance all the same. I have the opportunity to be a Black Wiccan and join in a spiritual partnership that fosters growth for everyone, especially for myself. I don't have to be afraid. As situations arise that are uncomfortable or fueled with misunderstanding or lack of acceptance, I am still on the path of growth within the world that the Goddess and God created for me. They created me to embody the shell and spirit of my ancestors through the pigment of my skin. I understand it and I am honored. I get to live this life rich in color and beauty, a descendant of the oldest in creation, connected by blood to the motherland and live as a black woman with pride. It is challenging at times; I understand it and it is love.

Stepping Out on Faith

Flame Bridhesdottir

Kinky hair, nose to there
Thick lips, hands on my hips.
Speaking out and Sunday shoutin'
Caramel skin, a goddess within
Rounded thighs, a woman outside
Big brown eyes, nothing to hide
Celtic pride along my Afro side
Give honor to the blessed Bride
Child of Nubia, standing tall
Daughter of Erin, hearing Her call.

Faith is the substance of things hoped for, the evidence of things unseen.
Hebrews 11:1

This is the beginning, I am four years old, and my mother is in tears. She's accidentally backed our enormous 1972 Chevrolet Bel-Air over Turk, one of a set of twin black cats we owned. Turk was a sweetheart, but entirely too trusting and unaware for a cat. I'm momentarily saddened, distressed more by my mother's tears than by any real feeling of loss. I'm very young; death is too abstract for me to process. Maybe my age renders me closer to the astral plane than the terrestrial anyway, and I haven't yet forgotten, so haven't learned to be afraid. At any rate, I wasn't the least bit surprised when Turk brushed past my ankles the next day, and butted his head into my hand, arching his back for a scratch.

I don't know if I ever told my mother about Turk's visit. It most likely never occurred to me that it was anything remarkable. How was I to know that dead was supposed to mean forever? In my mind, dead was the same as Cleveland; it was someplace you went, and then when you were done visiting, you came home.

Okay, that's not the beginning. This is the beginning; I am six, and I stay with my grandparents during the summer. My granddaddy is a minister, a lean man with a sunburned neck and forearms, a meticulously pressed suit, and a soft spot for animals, especially cats. My grandmother is plump, blue eyed, and when she's not in her nurse's uniform she can be spotted on Sunday in a dress befitting a preacher's wife, modest and usually pastel.

Today is Sunday and we are at church; or rather, we are in a converted barn that is spending this incarnation as a church. There are a lot of pastel dresses here, including my own. It's hot, my white tights are itchy, and my white patent mary janes pinch my toes.

The air is close with the smell of hymnals, old wood, and overheated congregates. The good part of church, the singing, is over and now it's time for my grandfather to preach. He's wordy, but kind of quiet for a preacher I think; not much like the TV preachers at all.

Just now, a bright green inch worm drops from the ceiling to the floor on a slender silver thread. I can no longer hear my granddaddy. I slide from the pew to my hands and knees and follow that inch worm, doggedly, painfully, slowly, but just as surely, right out the door of that church.

But maybe that's not the beginning either. Maybe it really all started when I was eight years old and had a severe asthma attack, and my granddaddy laid hands on me and prayed and I could suddenly breathe. And I believed.

Of course, it could just as easily have been when I was nine years old and discovered Greek mythology and read every tale I could get my hands on. And I believed.

When I saw the bobbing, dipping, zipping balls of light in my room, I instinctively knew not to tell anyone. But I believed.

I traveled between these two worlds; the sleepy church steeped rural world of my White grandparents and the impossibly fast moving, urban world that my White mother had chosen long before I was born. I saw my Marine father sometimes. He and my mother had divorced when I was very young, and so my memories of him are largely of a stern, handsome brown man who never really approved of me.

Thanks to the twisted attentions of a teen-aged boy with a fragmented soul, I learned to leave my body when I was five and by the time I was seven, I spent more time out of my *corpus* than in it. And so I grew up, walking two worlds, loved and hated in both, neither fully Black nor fully White, only fully on the outside looking in but always believing.

Despite my near constant immersion in the Christian church, I was fascinated by the occult from my earliest memories. I lived for horror movies, worshiped Vincent Price, and thought Yvonne DeCarlo as Lily Munster was beautiful beyond compare. I had a crush on Frank Langella that never fully went away. I pored through books of fantasy, horror, fairy tales and magic; but instead of finding them merely amusing, I felt if I just read enough of them I'd remember something very important that I had once known but had since forgotten. I mixed herbs and liquids, brewed "potions", but I never knew what I was trying to cure. And I believed.

In my teens I discovered the alchemy of cannabis, music, and sex. I believed in this magic like no other and followed the leather clad shamans and shawl draped priestesses of rock and roll with all the devotion of an initiate. *This* magic, this magic I could *do*. This was real and if I just listened hard enough, partied hard enough, fucked hard enough, I could almost remember the music I had once heard but had since forgotten; sometimes I could even be in my body and it was okay. So maybe this is where it truly began.

But what am I trying to say here? That I felt the pull of something wild and impossibly ancient? That the call came not just from the Dark Continent or the Emerald Isle but from the molten bones of Earth Herself and from the blackest reaches of the heavens?

Ah, but I di(pro)gress. The bubbling brew of sex, drugs, and rock and roll fueled my flights of fancy. I was the Fool of the Tarot; stepping blithely off into the unknown, confident that the Universe would catch me, and it always did. And I believed.

Eventually my path led to a man and that man led to two daughters. Suddenly my belief alone wasn't enough; I needed something more, something to protect my star seeds until they found their own belief. The dark magic of alcohol had turned on me, so I put down the chalice. No longer trusting my own magic, I turned to the Church, and threw myself into that institution as only a prodigal daughter will. Gone were the revealing clothes, the substances, the delicious and salacious. Instead there was Sunday school, potluck suppers, silent rebukes and denial. If you had listened then, you might have heard me dying. Whither the ecstatic spiritual experience? Wither the ecstatic spiritual experience. I wore a lot of pastel dresses, and I sang in the choir, and I dutifully tithed from the stash of dollars I kept hidden from my violent, crack smoking husband. But I didn't believe.

I was leaving my body again, often for days at a time. When I grew ill from the bacteria my crack addled, faithless husband deposited at the gate of my womb like Pandora's box, I at first didn't notice anything amiss. It was only when my children came to visit me in the hospital, barefoot, dirty, unkempt from their father's neglect, that I realized how close they had come to being motherless.

So this, this surely must be the beginning; That motherfucker had to go. That fucker of *this* mother, who defiled my holy vessel through his selfishness, who nearly killed me in his own brokenness, had to go. I could not heal him; but I could save myself. And so I believed.

I gathered up my star seeds, left behind my pastel dresses and that building unvisited by Yahweh; I took up painting, pottery, and peace, and movie nights with the magic number three of us piled in the recliner inches from the TV. During one of these movie marathons, hands full of red licorice, I began to cry while the end credits rolled on part one of the Lord of the Rings trilogy. My star seeds patted me with their candy sticky hands, proffering tissues. I had no explanation for my sudden tears, for the overwhelming wave of what could only be described as homesickness and longing. It was only after they went to bed that I could sit down to pinpoint the reason for my outburst. Upon rewatching the movie I identified the culprit. The sound track itself was causing my distress, specifically Enya singing "May It Be". Ah, music! Rather than soothing the breast of this savage it was instead rending it to pieces.

Soon I was getting misty anytime I heard Celtic music. Attempting to put an end to my emotional swings, I began researching meditation and relaxation techniques on the internet. Given my subject it was inevitable that I one day stumbled across a site on Wicca and witchcraft. I was thunderstruck. I stayed awake most of the night, feverishly clicking from link to link, website to website, my eyes, brain and soul drinking in the words on the screen. I now I had a name to put to my belief, my dreams, all the times I knew without knowing. Electrified, I stepped into my back yard, where by chance a full moon hung low in the velvety night sky. I fell to my knees and wept, this time in gratitude, whispering, "Thank You, thank You" over and over. I felt I had come home. And I believed.

And so this too was the beginning. The next year was full of discoveries, the most curious of which was the realization that Black folks weren't exactly thick on the ground in the Pagan community. Like many recent travelers on the Path, I made my first contacts in the community online, via internet discussion groups. I didn't upload a photo, being still nervous and protective of this new treasure, and seeking to guard my privacy from friends and family members who already thought me "eccentric". My first face to face contact with a local group bordered on the comical. As many groups do, a public meeting was arranged first. On the day of the big event,

I dressed carefully, as nervous as if this were a first date with an eligible bachelor. This was a family oriented group and I arrived at the pizza parlor with my star seeds, then two and five, in tow.

This is the beginning...of a spaghetti Western. Our hero walks into a saloon, and a hush falls. The needle scratches across the ragtime record on the Victrola in the corner, and the saloon patrons stare, mouths agape, before one of them drawls, "Yew ain't frum round heah, is yew boy?"

While not exactly that dramatic, the surprise on the faces of the group was certainly evident before being swept aside in the flurry of introductions to the fifteen people who had turned out to meet me. The fact that I didn't slink out at the first opportunity meant that I believed.

This led to another beginning, that of regular and loving contact with people who believed the same things I did, heard the same music I heard, and *remembered the things I had forgotten*. They held workshops and rituals, family game nights and outings. I saw many things that first year on my new path, but what I didn't see was anyone who looked like me. It was to be two more years before the cheeks that I kissed at the end of ritual came in any shade other than rosy pink.

Autumn Equinox 2006. Brighid has sent me a mate, and his children and my children are now our children. We are camping at a Pagan gathering and I set off on my own to attend a women's ritual. I spy her across the circle: skin like polished walnut, long black curls, so like my own mahogany spirals, spilling over her shoulders. In her simple white sheath and elaborate facial paint, she appears like Isis incarnate, serene and radiant. She slips away afterward and I excitedly run back to my campsite. Breathlessly, I tell my fiancé what I have seen. "Honey, I just saw another Black girl!" He stares at me a moment, wrinkling his Irish-ly freckled nose in confusion before slowly saying, "And?"

It hits me; everywhere he goes, he sees his face mirrored back to him. He doesn't get it. "Look around." I say. Comprehension slowly dawns across his features. There are easily 200 people in attendance at this event and I see him grasp the realization that this woman and I make up the entirety of a distinct minority *within* a minority. This apparently leaves quite an impression on him, as later he calls my attention to a young Black male who appears on the scene, apparently well known and liked by those present, bringing our numbers to the ever magical three. The three of us are like points on a triangle, defining the whiteness within, maintaining an equidistance at all times during the gathering, lest we accidentally get too close to one another and risk being identified with each other rather than with the group as a whole.

Or I could just be full of shit. It's far more likely that we were simply strangers to one another and our mutual blackness did not provide enough common ground upon which to strike up an acquaintance. Nevertheless, I now knew that I wasn't alone. And I believed.

When the Goddess sends you a mate it is *good*; improbably, impossibly, "oh-boy-is-this-for-me?!" good. So a year after the revelation at the campgrounds, the time came when my fiancé and I decided to legalize our union. While not Pagan himself, my living breathing Pan enthusiastically supported my desire to have a full blown Wiccan handfasting. Through a friend we found a high priestess licensed to solemnize marriages in our state. We agreed to meet at a truck stop halfway between our two towns.

We spotted her quickly and made our way over to her table. As we crossed the room, I noticed her face looked odd, as if it couldn't quite decide what expression to wear and so was stuck in a loop of conflicting reactions. She greeted us brusquely and motioned to the seats across the table. She wore her kinky curly black hair pulled loosely back; her sea green eyes, so like my mother's, regarding me coolly across the Formica tabletop. Stunned by her resemblance to a young version of my mother, (indeed, to all the women on that side of my family) I asked where in the United States her family was from, apologizing for staring. I explained that she bore a striking resemblance to the women on my mother's side and she stiffened, drawing herself up and back in the plastic chair. "I'm Irish." she flatly declared. When I exclaimed over her eyes and how like my mother's they were, she leaned in toward me, anger blazing in their depths and in a low voice snapped, "I'm Irish!" with a finality that made me blink. "So is my mother." I said, the intensity of her anger leaving me momentarily befuddled. Her shoulders relaxed a bit but for the remainder of our appointment she was stern and businesslike.

Later that week I visited the friend who had recommended the High Priestess. I described our strange encounter to Rose, exclaiming "I don't know what I said wrong, but I really offended her somehow." Rose bustled around the table where I sat nursing a mug of coffee, her eyes averted from mine. Finally she faced me, took a deep breath and said, "She thought you were implying she was Black" with the flat, toneless certainty of those who reluctantly must relay unpleasant truths. My mouth gaped and my eyebrows shot into my hairline. Rose looked chagrined on behalf of the entire White race. "How do you know? Did she say something to you?" I choked out in disbelief. "No, it's just..." and now she looked really sheepish, "it's just that I know how people..." (What people? Do I know these people? My brain was reeling.) "I know how people are. And you said when you told her your mom was Irish she backed off."

Rose now looked as if she'd rather be on the astral than standing there having this conversation with me; she did not relish being the person that ripped the love and light veil from my love affair with all things Pagan. This was a beginning as well. I took my first step toward understanding the Shadow, and thus duality. And still, I believed.

Fortunately disillusion does not hinder the turning of the Wheel and my life passed in relative contentment, notwithstanding personal, family, and financial crises. I found myself with the opportunity and the funds to attend a festival put together by none other than the aforementioned High Priestess. We had gone ahead with our plans to have her officiate our handfasting and I doggedly attempted to strike up a friendship with her. My efforts failed but whether this was due to her issues, or the reemergence (Emergency! My soul is in peril!) of my alcoholism, I've never been able to discern. Nevertheless, I attended the festival, my first since I "discovered" other Black Pagans.

Through benefit of my membership in a large online Pagan community, I now regularly conversed with other Pagans of Color, one of whom I arranged to meet in person at the festival. We greeted each other like old pals, before drifting apart to set up camp. As I walked to my site, I wryly noted that there was one other Black person in attendance, a guy who was a member of the band that would play later that night. This was in clear compliance with that unwritten Universal Law which states that no more than three Black people may be present at any given Pagan gathering.

As my husband and I wandered about, socializing and checking out vendors, we made the acquaintance of a pleasant older couple in the vendor's area. While we chit-chatted, it came out that the wife of the couple was a Santera, an initiated priestess of Santeria. She asked me about my path and when I told her I honored a Celtic deity, she wondered, like many people I meet, why I didn't follow any of the African religio-magic paths. I was taken aback. I replied that I had never really thought about it, Brighid had called and I had never looked back. I had no pull toward the African paths. To myself I thought, "And who is this White lady to question me anyway? I could just as easily ask her why she wasn't passing the drinking horn at an Asatru sumbel!"

They served us some of the mead they crafted and talk eventually turned to other things. Presently we parted from our gracious hosts to partake in the various festivities around the campgrounds.

This is the beginning...of madness. The ringing tones of a djembe are heard, and the band launches into the first of a series of driving tribal songs, all powered by the heavy drum beats. The mead is really hitting me now, (emergence-y!) and I move into the area in front of the stage, turning, dipping, swaying, jumping; Africa in my hips and feet if nowhere else. The rest of the night passes in this fashion, broken only by hasty gulps of mead taken between rounds of frenzied dancing. I rip my watch off and throw it into the bonfire, screaming "FUCK TIME!" before launching myself back into the throbbing waves of sound. Behold! Hither the ecstatic experience!

The next morning, head aching, we go in search of the couple from the night before to bid them goodbye and thank them for their excellent mead, company, and wisdom. The campgrounds have those low down, mean mistreatin' post party blues, soggy and quiet as everyone packs up to return to the mundane world. I greet the woman while my husband says farewell to her husband in typical manly fashion; he helps break down their vending tent. The men thus engaged, she pulls me to the side, looks earnestly into my face and urgently says, "I have a message for you." I blink. "From who?" I ask, losing my grammatical grasp in my surprise. "From the Ancestors. There is something they wish you to know." Oh boy, here we go with the Africa stuff again. "Tell the Ancestors I said 'thanks but no thanks.' I'm not interested." I say, sounding ill-mannered even to my hung-over ears. I soften my tone, "Really, I just don't feel any pull in that direction, so I'd rather not have the obligation that would come with the receipt of the message. I am not ready for that level of commitment." I chuckle a bit, embarrassed at my rudeness, hoping to gloss over the insult. Fortunately for me she is not offended, instead regarding me as one would an exceptionally thick headed child who is nonetheless kind of cute. She hugs me, shaking her head and laughing softly to herself.

This is the beginning... of healing. After my mead fueled

trance dance I could no longer deny that I had strayed back onto the left hand path of my alcoholism. I threw myself into recovery and in the process experienced profound and rapid spiritual growth of a kind I hadn't known since my first stumbling faery dusted steps on the Path. It was during this process that I developed a sudden (and quite rabid) interest in hoodoo, an African-American system of folk magic. Surprised at my own self, I contacted my would-be messenger of a year prior. My e-mail to her simply stated, "I'm ready to hear now. What did They say?" Almost immediately I received an equally simple reply. "They said your path lies in the African traditions." I stared at my monitor and laughed. But this time, I believed.

Two months later I'm having coffee with a new friend of mine, a local clairvoyant with whom I share an easy rapport. As we're chatting, sipping our coffees and munching scones, he suddenly looks at me curiously, abruptly stopping me in mid-sentence to urgently say, "I need to ask you something." "Sure, lay it on me." I say expansively. "Do you practice Vodou, or any of the African paths?" Sheesh! What is it with White people and Africa? "No. I'm really getting into hoodoo, but it's not Vodou and not a religion either. It's a system of folk magic. Why do you ask?" He carefully wraps the remainder of his scone in a napkin before answering. "Because when I looked at you just now, I saw a white turban on your head. Not the Middle Eastern kind but the large African head wrap." This prompts me to tell him about my conversation and subsequent e-mail with the Santera and my admission that my curiosity is starting to get the better of me, which ends with me wondering aloud, "...but where the fuck would I even find a Vodou practitioner in this town?" We both laugh at this and talk turns to lighter subjects. I return home jazzed on caffeine and good company, and pensive.

I've been walking two worlds for so long that I'm beginning to think that *is* my path. The Black, the White, the dark, the light, the day, the night; the thump of the bodhrán merging seamlessly with the ringing beat of the djembe, and me in the middle, dancing to the ancient rhythm. I don't know where my path will end, but I do know how it started.

This is the beginning: I am one hour old and my mother is gazing raptly at my amber skin and dark eyes, touching the silky down on my head. The nurse asks her what my name is and with the age old magic, my mother speaks me into being. "Her name is Faith." And I believe.

Tapestry of the Soul

Luna Pantera

Gentle caress, baby powdered smells.
Godmother who always smelled of Lavender and chocolate chip
cookies.
Times in the Garden talking to the flowers, vegetables, fey.
Witches spells can cure and heal.
But be careful who you tell.
Not everyone can do what we do.
They wouldn't understand.

Godmother's heart is sick.
She has to go away for a while.
I have to go where the energy doesn't feel right.
I'm scared.
Mommie don't leave me here!
I promise to be good!
Take me with you!

I'm alone with the man who always talks about God and sin.
Breathe.
Godmother says the only sin is in the hearts of men who always talk
about sin.
Breathe.

Cuddling is nice.
Breathe.
Like when godmother and I have cookies and tea in little jade cups
and take naps together.
Breathe.

That doesn't feel right.
No! Stop!
No! No! No!
Please! Please!
Stop! Stop!
It hurts!

I want my mommie!
I'm scared.
Breathe.
Breathe.
Pain/Shame. Pain/Shame.
Breathe.
Breathe.
No one will believe you.
Your nothing but a crybaby.
Silly little girl.
You asked for it.
You wanted it.
You deserved it.
You deserved it.
Breathe.
Breathe.

I wake up.
I remember, but I pretend it was a bad dream.
Dreams can't hurt you.
Dreams aren't real.
I go into the living room.

Everyone is there.
The god man.
Breathe.
His wife.
Breathe.
My Mommie.
Something bad is going to happen.

How could you?
He's a man of God!
You're evil!
Say it!
I'm not evil.
He is.
Mommie no!
Stop hitting me.
I'm not evil.
I'm not evil.
Please stop.

Mommie please believe me.
Mommie believe me.
I'm evil!
I'm evil!
I'm evil!
Breathe.
Breathe.
Breathe.

I'm almost perfect now.
The size three is getting too big for me now.
The guy I met at the club drives a Porsche.
A Porsche!
That's cool right?
I'll knock him out with my Charles Jordan spike heels and Taharie
dress.
Hair, nails, make up perfect!

Dinner must have cost a fortune.
The wine was so sweet, warm and tasty.
Another glass wouldn't hurt.
Wow!
A pent house on Nob Hill.
What a view!

Kissing is nice.
Breathe.
Ok, we can sit on the couch.
I can't breathe.
Breathe.
Breathe.
I can't scream.
He's too strong.
I try to scream again…but it gets stuck in my throat.
N…
Breathe.
Breathe.
Breathe.
Just lie still it will be over soon.

Tears run down my cheeks…between my legs.
Was it good for you?

He sees the tears.
Fear and guilt set in.
You weren't that good anyway.
Breathe.
Breathe.
Breathe.

Years go by of pain and shame.
Pain and shame.
No real love.
Only false passion.
You're not good enough.
You don't deserve true love…real passion.
You're not good enough.
You don't deserve…The pain is too much
I want it to go away.
I need it to go away!
Razor stings a brief moment.
Redden wrist.
Release.
Release.
Release.
Numbness/Darkness…

Stop!!!
What do you think you're doing there girl?
Haven't you heard me crying with you?
Calling you to me?
Come to me now and stop this foolishness!
Are you the light?
Light?!!!
Girl, you got to give up that Christian tomfoolery!
But if you need light…
The darkness fades slowly away.
Replaced with a dark red, then orange and finally yellow light.
The taste of honey fills my mouth.
Slips down my throat.
Warmth spreads throughout my body.
My spirit lightens.
My heart dances with memories of joy, completeness, and divinity.
I feel myself turn around and behind me I see a mirror.
I go to touch it.

Luna Pantera

Beautiful woman.
Carmel brown skin.
Big brown eyes filled with such compassion and love.
I can help but cry with longing.
I touch the mirror with my tears and it disappears.
She is me and I am Her.
I have called you and waited so long for you to answer my call.
Strong, beautiful arms reach out and beckon me.
I go and She pulls me into her bosom.
And I cry and She cries.
My tears mixed with Hers and together they become an ocean.
And together we wash away all the pain and shame of all the years.
Cobwebs that have smothered my soul melt away.
I cry until I don't believe I have any more tears to shed.
I am at peace and rest gently in the bosom of the Mother.
I still my breath and I feel peace.
There is more.
No!
I don't want it!
You need to heal.
I am healed enough!
I'm fine as I am!
You are incomplete.
It's time to take back what was stolen from you.
What was lost is found.
I take a breath.
Ask her to hold me in her arms.
A kiss to the third eye and I am back.

There is nowhere to go.
I hear them coming.
The door is kicked down.
The light goes out.
I hear the scream of anguish of my beloved, as he knows he cannot
save me.
I feel his spirit leave this plane.
I fight, but there are too many of them.

Witch.
Devil's whore.
Make her pay.
Make her pay.

Blood runs down bruised thigh.
An emptiness spreads across my belly.
Her name was to have been Brigid.

Torn and broken body dragged through the town.
Beg for mercy and death will be swift.
You can't kill me...I'm already dead.
Body thrown on burning twigs.
No physical pain can match the pain in my soul.
You can't kill me...I'm already dead.
You can't kill me...I'm already dead.
You can't kill me...I'm already dead.

I come back in a river under a waterfall.
Tears I thought were done run freely.
I become a living waterfall.
So much pain.
So much lost.
Why did you show me?
It's time to Reclaim what has been ripped from your soul.
You are ready.
No!!!
The gifts come with a price that's too high!
I'm not willing to pay the toll!
Do you think it has always been like this?
Close your eyes.
No!
Close your eyes!
You can't have darkness without sun.
Pain without pleasure.
Now close your eyes!
It's hard to hold out with an Orisha.
They can wait for years, decades, lifetimes.

So, I close my eyes.
And I'm in a temple so beautiful human words can't describe it.
Marble sculptures.
Fine incense and spices fill the air.
Beautiful woman who are bathed and oil and worshiped for the
Priestess they are.
Trained in the art of pleasure.
All acts of love and pleasure are my rituals.

Men are humbled in this place.
They know it is the closest thing to Deity they will experience while
of human breath.
Every caress, kiss, act of pleasure invokes Deity into other.
This is yours to Reclaim too.
There are different types of healing.
And all are sacred to me.

Now is the time.
You are ready.
You are strong.
You have paid the toll.
Kiss me.
Now a kiss from the Goddess is nothing to take lightly.
Just ask some of the other Orisha.
But by now a kiss seemed easier than arguing with Her for a few
more years…lifetimes.
I take a deep breath.
Close me eyes.
And accept the Kiss of Oshun.

I breathe into you.
Healer.
Fiery Lover.
Warrior.
Poet.
Beauty.
And Sacred Whore.
You are my daughter.
Own what has always been yours and always will be.

Memories are like threads that connect to our soul.
We can go through many lifetimes of stumbling on them.
Or we can weave a beautiful tapestry of our choosing.
Pain/Shame.
Guilt/Blame.
Joy/Love.
Lose/Hope
Can all be used in the design.
A Tapestry of Change.
A Tapestry of Growth.
A Tapestry of the Soul

A Tapestry of the Soul.
A Tapestry of the Soul.

Let the healing continue.
Let the healing begin.

I Need More Feet

Janet Callahan

I need more feet. My mother says that she often feels like she has one foot in each world. For her those worlds are the "white" world (the mainstream normal world where she lives and works, and is working on a PhD in social work), and the Native American world (the world of her family – her life at home and her upbringing). My mom is Lakota, an enrolled member of the Oglala Sioux Tribe, and grew up in a somewhat traditional family, even if they were Christian.

Growing up in a house with her and my very narrow minded (and white) father, I often felt that way too – I was walking with one foot in her world, and one foot in his. As an adult I have one foot in the white world, where I live and work and function day in and day out. I have another foot in the Native American world - I'm finally listed on the rolls myself, as is my young son, making us "real" Indians according to the government. But to add to the confusion, I also have a foot in the Pagan world. And while a three legged stool may be more stable than one with only two legs, it doesn't make for a very stable personal life some days.

When I told my mother I was leaving the church of my childhood, she wanted to make sure I still believed that murder was wrong and other basic moral tenants. When I told her my artwork, which up to that time, was exclusively traditional Native American in style and focusing on beadwork, was branching out into the metaphysical; the line between the two worlds became clear. My mother asked me specifically to keep these things separate; separate websites or separate sales channels or something because "that" (Paganism) is "not Indian."

So I have, for the most part. Keeping these parts of my life separate though, is sometimes like that game kids play sometimes with bamboo poles that are hit together and then on the ground with a person jumping in and out from between them. The game is called tinikling, for anyone who sat there for a bit like I did wondering what that game is called. I already have one foot grounded pretty firmly in the mainstream world most days, so my remaining foot is hopping back and forth over this line between Pagan and Native.

Most of the time I'm pretty successful at keeping them separate, though it takes a lot of thinking and planning. Other times I land wrong and the bamboo poles smash my ankle; using beadwork skills to make ritual jewelry was one that caused a stir, for example.

In the Pagan community we often talk about what "path" we're on, by which we mean which specific variety of Pagan we are. In Native American communities there's talk of the "Red Road", the life that is in line with traditional ways, beliefs, and thought patterns. Some days I manage to walk on just one road with a nice steady gait...and others, I trip, stumble, and jump around from pathway to pathway. On the best days I dance between them all with beauty and grace.

One thing that must be understood, the Red Road is not so much a religion or a faith but is a way of interacting with the world around us. It encompasses every aspect of life: the way we interact with the environment, the way we interact with each other, the way we interact with the divine. It's a way of treating people and a way of living in harmony. While the details vary from tribe to tribe, it is generally based on tribal living and tribal viewpoints and the good of society over individual goals. Each tribe has their own language and their own mythologies and culture, making for many different interpretations of the details. There is no one single "Native American Religion," though there is an organization called the Native American church which is based around peyote, a plant found in certain areas in the southwest United States.

So then, what's the difference between stumbling all over my three feet and dancing gracefully? A lot of times what makes me stumble are the things I encounter along the way. Most of the time, when I encounter something in the mainstream world that doesn't match up with either the Native American or the Pagan worlds, or even is actively hostile towards them, I can write it off fairly easily as racism, classism, sexism, or just plain ignorance. The few issues that come up in the Native American world are the same issues that I've had there since childhood, so they are known hazards. It's the Pagan world that gives me the most difficulties.

Don't get me wrong, I try to be polite. More than once I've left a workshop, ritual, or other event rather than argue with the person in charge about their deeply held beliefs about Native Americans. In the grand scheme of things there are probably better options but since it's hard to tell who really wants to learn and who is convinced that their spirit guide or their former life is the absolute truth, and it's easier to walk away.

Sometimes it's the perspective of those not familiar with Native American perspectives that trips me up. Have you ever seen or read a totem dictionary? The whole idea of a totem dictionary didn't make sense to me for a long time. While there are stories about different animals and how they might help people, not all tribes have the same concept of those animals or even the concept of a personal totem. Further, why would you look up an animal's strengths when knowing what they do or asking them when you encounter them is a little more traditional.

Sometimes I run across things, however, that border on or even cross the line into outright fraud. It really makes me question the level of spiritual practice of the people who do this sort of thing because it is a misuse of a way of being that was never theirs to begin with. To make a syncretic whole of the Pagan and Indian worlds requires understanding them both and that's not something you can do when you start with a fraudulent foundation. It makes tripping over your own feet more likely when you try to walk that ever-shifting path.

I recently was exposed to a local group, for example, who told the assembled group of prospective seekers that they did sweat lodges as part of their program. They were quick to assure us they weren't like that "fake" one out in Arizona, motivational speaker James Arthur Ray, who had people die in a sweat at a new age retreat center. After all, they'd learned from *real* Indians, and knew how to do it **right**. Though, apparently, "right" for them meant that they'd learned about sweats from men, and then they'd adapted the teachings to be specific to women.

Adapted? What does that mean in this context? How can they be doing it "right" if they're changing what they learned?

Further discussion lead to another major red flag for me , this particular group charges a large sum of money (more than $1000) for their several month long seeker class. In traditional Lakota ways one doesn't charge for a sweat. In fact, in traditional Native American ways of pretty much all tribes, one doesn't charge for a sweat. Even in many Pagan groups, charging for teaching is not acceptable. That made this whole situation against the principles of both paths that they claimed to represent, which left me wondering about their motives.

With a few more questions we learned that their teachings were a mixture of Eastern philosophies and a specific "Native American" group who has been widely publicized as "plastic shamans", frauds, and not Native American at all. So here we have a group claiming to be real, learning from a group who is well known to not be real.

Other warning signs for this group included the fact that all of this discussion was done in sacred space, which they made without really explaining what they were doing. My very first Pagan mentor taught me that it was rude to bring someone into a ceremony or ritual without their consent – that we always have the option of not circling with someone we're not sure of or uncomfortable with.

Even though we had each been provided with a form to fill out with our intentions, to be provided to them privately at the end, the leaders seemed to want to leverage people into making a decision right then and there. Towards the end of the evening the organizer went around the circle, asking whether we thought we'd participate. They made it very clear that if we valued ourselves, we'd find a way to pay for this; no matter what our financial state was. Here in Michigan many families are struggling to keep a roof over their heads and food on the table for their families. I have a special needs child and I knew I could not commit the time required for their program. I was told that putting my family's sanity first was tantamount to not caring about myself.

Between my need to balance my family's life, and my growing distaste for the philosophies the group presented, I quietly declined the honor of joining them and went home to re-think my involvement in the local community yet again.

So, where does that leave me? Mostly it leaves me still trying to find a balance point between the three worlds I walk in every day. As time goes by I get better at it but I still tend to trip when others try to blur the lines between those worlds. From time to time, I wonder what damage we'll see come from those attempts – especially as Native groups gain more access to the internet to see things that are being done in their names.

Missing in the Picture

Olivia Haynes

'I wish there were more Black people here.' It's a common thought I always have when I attend festival after festival, metaphysical shop after metaphysical shop. Again, I am the fly in the milk and hating it. I wish there were more Blacks in Paganism - or at least more out of the broom closet because the African American culture is still gripped by Christianity mainly and Islam second. I figured I could enjoy myself more because I would have people I can actually talk to and joke with rather than paint on a smile and find a corner to count the hours with. I do enjoy the idea of going to Pagan events; it's just being there is the daunting part. I may as well be in an empty room instead of being surrounded by the people I'm not going to connect easily with.

I'm very happy being Pagan, very happy. I was raised non-denominational Christian (so I still don't understand denominational squabble, regardless of religion or lack-thereof) but I switched over to Paganism around 15 or 16 years old. Becoming Pagan was not an easy transition since I was Black and raised in the inner city, it was not expected of me nor of the norm to be of any religion that was not Christian or at least Afrocentric Muslim. Mentions of Black Buddhists, Black Jews or even Black atheists were barely ever heard of because of the self-defeating depiction of mainstream Black culture where only the most cookie cutter and stereotypical survive. How you were supposed to act as a Black person was usually reinforced with "Black people don't do [whatever have you]." Apparently Black people don't get depressed, join non-Abramic religions, dress goth or punk or listen to rock music. There are so many little unwritten rules for being "Black", it is a very conservative but complex race. It seems anything can remove Blackness as if it were a loose leaf in the wind or being Black was a life-crippling ailment rather than a multi-ethnic race full of various cultures and rich backgrounds. Venture too far out the narrow lines and you're automatically deemed "White" or an "oreo": Black on the outside, White on the inside. I may be 23 and have dealt with blatant racism from other races but being despised by your own race hurts the most.

The lack of racial cultural support can be really crippling.

Sometimes my White Pagan friends wonder why I prefer Black Pagans around me more and there I see clearly the identity issues and social pressures they never really had to deal with. As a minority within a nation that has plenty of disdain towards it and is not as post-racism as people would like to believe, it is a fine line to walk when stepping outside of the monolith. To be a minority within another minority, it is like becoming an Untouchable or trapped in social solitary. To other Blacks, you're seen as a defect of the race since you're not upholding the "values" of Blackness, as warped and misguided as some of those values may be. To Whites, they really don't know how to take you but it seems flocking to closet racist jokes are almost the first thing done. To feel alone like this, it is nearly no wonder how many Black Pagans feel depressed and isolated.

I am raised in the inner city – the ghetto, the hood, whatever you want to call it; I called it home. I am happily Black, for it is my race and I have pride of our historical accomplishments. However, my background does make it difficult to socialize with White Pagans who are most likely middle class and the most they know of the inner city is whatever the news and movies tell them. I cannot truly relate nor do I want a painfully suburban middle class life and because the responses I get are very cringe-worthy. I do not like my culture treated as farce and I especially hate it when I am greeted with very poor Black slang from someone who knows less than three Black people. It does annoy me greatly when a White Pagan says "Oh, I know how you feel with persecution" or "Slavery was over in the 1800s, you're not persecuted against anymore! I, however, still have to still deal with problems because I'm Pagan and a woman living in a patriarchal society!" I'm Black, Pagan, was raised in the inner city and a woman; give me a break. That has taught me that no matter how open minded the religion, ignorance can still flourish. I don't like being asked about why Black people do this or that. The easiest answer is make friends with Black people, we're not lab rats to be studied. I prefer to talk about normal Black culture with other Black Pagans, share jokes about Black culture and talk about the Black condition without close-minded commentary from someone who doesn't understand. In being around other Black Pagans there is the feeling that we're still Black and that we're normal amongst ourselves, there's solidarity. We can talk about things in Black culture, media, press and livelihoods. We can joke about our stereotypes and how to combat them, being Black in America and our run-ins with Black Christianity. It's not separation

I want; it's the normalcy I'm after.

I used to have something like that, the normalcy. When I started in Paganism, there was one Black metaphysical shop that I would go to all the time and hang out. The owner was Black, the workers were Black, there were accurate portrayals of Egyptian gods, extensive products for those who practiced Vodun/Voodoo and Santeria, it was in a Black neighborhood, the customers were mostly Black. There was always somebody chatting about Black issues such as police in America, laws, the lack of genuine diversity in Paganism and the misused popularity of the Egyptian pantheon. It was possibly the most normal I ever felt in Paganism because it was people who looked like me, was raised in the same cultural background as I was and I could relate to them. Our store was normal; we attracted the philosophers who were entrenched in the notion of Black power. I remember one summing up music, culture, religion and the arts: "Black people make it, White people take it". We had Black conspiracy theorists, masons, Afrocentric witches, wise women and occasionally the raving Black Christian. It was just a Black metaphysical shop. Then after a couple tumultuous years the shop closed and everyone dispersed. I didn't have a place to really call home anymore. Thankfully it was after my learning years so I wouldn't take on a nasty racial complex about my identity but still it sucks feeling like a cultural refugee.

I miss being able to chat about Chris Rock, Louis Farrakhan and Spike Lee movies, marvel at how well Denzel Washington emulated Malcolm X perfectly, if Obama will do well in office as an American president and as the first Black president, and where is Jay-Z's career going in a non-politically correct world. I personally believe that just like there is a Black Christianity as opposed to an all-encompassing Christianity, there is also a separate Black Paganism that is different from the usual staple White Paganism because our backgrounds are different. We still believe in the same things but interpret them differently. We integrate the cultures that we were raised with in them. Paganism combined with Black culture is going to herald a different outcome from Paganism combined with White culture.

If there is one thing to note, Black Christianity makes being a Black Pagan incredibly difficult. Black Christianity is very feverish, stout, extremely conservative and does exude a bit of Stockholm Syndrome. In my experience, Black Christians either assumed I was without God or praying to the Devil and always would they be quick to tell me that Christ will deliver me from my religion and back to the one I was originally unhappy with, Christianity, because it is righteous. I have gotten fairly mild responses but they can grow quickly vicious so other Black Pagans simply learn hymns, go to church every Sunday and fake it. It's either that or be disowned or harmed by the family and/or community. We see what happens to Black gays and we're very well aware we Black Pagans won't receive better treatment and may possibly get worse treatment. Black Christianity is firmly embedded in Black culture, humor, and life, and to ignore it or strongly rebel against it would not prove fruitful. Instead it is only best to toe outside of the broom closet when possible and merely gather online or to greet the ignorance head-on.

There are different varieties of Pagans out there because of their backgrounds and races. I like being around people of as many different backgrounds as I can find but I also appreciate a home base just like anyone else. People may pride themselves on being non-conformist but who really wants to be truly out casted from everything that they knew? I'm happy being Pagan and I'm proud to be Black, I just wish there was more Black Pagans around.

Minorities in the Pagan Community

Storm Kelley

Sisters of the Coventry
©2007 All Rights Reserved.
Sisters of the Coventry

All for one and one for thee
Each together circle 'round
Giving thanks from sky to ground
Sending energy high above
In perfect trust and perfect love
Calling Earth, Air, Fire, and Water
Powers of the Mother and Father
Celebrating the Sabbat days
Honoring all the ancient ways
Chanting to give our words flight
Empowered by the Full Moon's light
Hand in hand we'll always be
Sisters of the Coventry!

The Pagan Community is a very diverse group of individuals that have similar beliefs that do not conform to the mainstream religious paths accepted by society. This brings together many unique personalities from various backgrounds with a common interest – the Freedom of Religion.

Typically, the Pagan Community is not really a community at all but rather a collection of small groups within the community that operate on their own and by their own accord. They do not come together as a whole unit. The small groups vary in their beliefs and daily and ritual practices, sometimes resulting in the inability to accept beliefs that differ from that particular group's ways. These groups usually have a closed network that the community, as a whole, does not have a great deal of information available to provide to anyone looking to learn about the pagan path (a.k.a. newbies). The community is supposed to be about educating the public about the truth and reality of Pagans and Witchcraft, however, since many of these groups are so closed to the public, there does not appear to be much educating taking place.

Many of the small groups hold their own private and "public" rituals for some of the Sabbats where a newbie can attend to see how the rituals are performed by the different groups and paths. It has been my experience that the public rituals are usually attended by community members that already know each other or members of the hosting group. There is rarely any educating being conducted about the ritual or group information, brochures, newsletters, or other forms of handouts available for anyone new to pagan community to read. The only form of education that I have witnessed has been for children under 12 years of age but nothing for anyone over the age of thirteen. A few attendees might introduce themselves to the newbies and introduce the newbie to a few other attendees from their personal circle; however, most attendees are not very forthcoming and tend to talk amongst themselves.

This type of community is difficult for any new learner attempting to find guidance and information about the pagan paths, but this is twice as hard on a minority person that comes to any event within the pagan community. A minority person may have even less contact at a public event with community members and part of this may be non-minority pagans being unsure of how to approach a minority pagan. It has been my own personal experience that it seems as if community members tend to avoid a minority person at an event a little more than a non-minority attendee. I have attended many events with non-minorities who had also never attended a public event before and found that community members would speak to my friends without giving me a second glance. I noticed that some attendees directed all of their conversation or questions at the non-minority newbies even though we stood side-by-side. This may be unintentional and it could be that some pagans assume that a minority attendee is either tagging along with a non-minority pagan or that the minority pagan only follows a path of Voodoo or Black Magic. The exchange of phone numbers, email addresses, or social networking website information seem to be enthusiastically extended to the non-minorities to maintain contact but others are a bit more hesitant to provide this information to a minority pagan. Almost every member of the pagan community will attest, as I found out, that they are not bigots or racists, and this may very well be true in most cases. I have not encountered many outright racist pagans in the community, but even one can set the tone for a minority pagan's attitude, view of participating in public events or socializing.

I want to share one incident, which I experienced, that made me aware that the pagan community is not immune to racism: A friend, a non-minority, informed me that "we" had been invited to attend a Samhain rite at a community member's home. We went with our kids – everyone's kids were going to be there – and our pot luck dishes; everything went great in the beginning! At one point after the ritual, there was an incident involving sharing turns on a video game system and my kids were being blamed by the host's child of doing something. There was something about the story that just did not seem quite right to me because the act my child was accused of was just not a behavior my child would do since he was too timid and never aggressive with anyone. Since I have experienced many incidents of racial stereotyping over my lifetime, from the looks, the women that grab their purses or move them to their other side away from me, to being followed around a store through every aisle; I decided to have my kids stay by me the rest of the time and we stayed in the kitchen. After awhile of standing in the kitchen area with not one person speaking to me and constantly receiving strange looks when my children or I would get something to eat; I informed my friend to that we were ready to leave. The following day, my non-minority friend commented that the host had made a comment to her that they "do not normally have *those people* in her home!" I could not fathom that I was actually hearing that racism was prevalent amongst pagans. I was under the belief that, since pagans are constantly discriminated against, the pagan community was the one group I thought would rise above this ludicrous mentality and accept everyone who chose to walk this path with open arms! I felt exiled, hurt, embarrassed, small, less worthy, and I felt as if everyone at the house was laughing at me because I did not know that my kids and I should not be there. I was livid mainly because if I had known this in the beginning, I would not have wasted my time or energy going to a place where I was not welcome and I would never willingly subject my kids to the mistreatment of bigots. I posted a comment to the pagan Yahoo group about how I felt about this incident. The host and a few of her friends called me a liar and argued that she was not racist and they did not hear anything. I learned by experience the emotional turmoil that a minority pagan feels when subjected to mean spirited pagans. I removed my membership from this group and at that point, I had decided that I would never enter a circle with people I did not know personally.

Although I feel that the majority of pagans in the community are very open and accepting of all other pagans, this incident caused me to be extremely untrusting of meeting new pagans in any community and to not want to attend public or private events again! I remained involved and became friends with a closed circle of pagans and my best friend was with me. I was the only minority member and it did not seem to be an issue for any of the other members. This closed circle formed a coven and things were great for the first two years. Sometime during the second year, things began to fall apart. The members began to gossip and it seemed many of them were on power-trips. I felt like I was amongst a group of childish, high school drama queens fighting over petty issues, jealousy, and popularity being the focus of many members, including my best friend - who then turned on me and, even to this day, goes out of her way to bad mouth me to other pagans and non-pagans alike. The group and the members became something I did not want to be a part of any longer so I stepped out and stopped participating in the group's activities. Since these incidents, I have rarely, if ever, attend any open or public rituals and have opted to remain a drama-free Solitary Pagan. I have been relatively content over the last five years. However, recently I have begun to attend a few festivals and open myself up to making new friends - but now I am just a little more selective about whom I allow into my Circle of Trust!

Despite the denials of its existence, this type of behavior is very much alive in the pagan community. Based on my experience, I feel that there is a lack of trust felt by some minority pagans in the pagan community and therefore we tend to keep to ourselves and do not have much contact with anyone outside our close, personal friends and family circle. This is a broken system that needs to be corrected in order to unite the pagan community as a whole and effectively promote religious freedom for all pagans. Unfortunately, as long as there are bigots and pagans in denial within our own pagan communities; this treatment will obviously not change any time soon and will continue to separate the community.

Although I am a Solitary Pagan and take pleasure in my solitude, I am still interested in making new pagan friends - and especially minority pagan friends! I can count on one hand how many minority pagans I know - and by "know" I mean in person or online! I believe that all minority pagans need to network with each other and come together to form a stronger community bond by meeting up and attending public events together or hold their own gatherings! The minority pagan community should come together, stand strong, and be vigilant on educating all new minority pagans so they have support within an already persecuted community and do not have to continue walking through the same struggles or feelings of loneliness on the Sister Path. In the spirit of solidarity, reach out to your fellow minority pagans. We are strong; we are beautiful, we are survivors, we are Mothers, we are Women, we are pagans, we are Sisters!

Saints, Goddesses, Voodoo! Oh My!

Gloria Jean

The year was 1956. I entered my earth journey as a Triple Pisces. I was born in the midst of a mystical city – New Orleans. This was a watery wonderland, where spirit flowed easily and created magick and mystery alongside the normal everyday hustle of life. Beauty and genteel southern manners existed side by side with racism and depravity. Darkness and light existed together on so many levels.

I was born to a Mexican-American mother and a Southern father from Mississippi – both of whom were trying to escape their heritages bestowed upon them during this lifetime. My father escaped his small country town by joining the Air Force. While stationed in California, he met my mother, who had promised herself that she would never fall into the life to which Mexican girls all seemed destined – to be a wife and mother. She had put herself through nursing school and had a career, although her family reminded her that she should not pass up a chance to be married and have a family. This was what society expected of women in the 1950s. My father went to war and, after a four-year long-distance courtship, my mother succumbed to society's pressures and married my father. She moved across the country to be married and settle in New Orleans, which was where my father had a teaching job. In this different land, she was not looked upon as being "Mexican", but more as an exotic person from another place. Here she could escape her heritage. My father escaped his by marrying into another culture and majoring in the Spanish language in college, which is what he would teach.

I was an extremely sensitive child - too sensitive for this world. I never felt any different ethnically in my world because New Orleans contains much diversity. Many of my classmates were of French and Italian descent, and we all shared the same basic coloring and features. Therefore, I never felt "different" in that way. We were raised in a typical Southern household: very strict parents, we ate Southern food (although with an occasional trip to Manuel's hot tamale stand, which was greasy but hot and tasty). That and the occasional Mexican dish that my mother prepared, always lamenting the difficulty of it, was the extent of the food of my mother's culture that we knew.

I was baptized and brought up in my mother's religion, which was Catholic. I was sent to Catholic school for four years. I found the religion class to be very difficult, nothing I could really relate to. Much of it was in Latin at the time, and we spent a lot of time reciting memorized prayers.

My third grade teacher was from Ireland. She regularly talked about doing penance in Ireland by sitting with her legs in waters infested with electric eels. She also talked about the fairies and leprechauns. She truly believed in them. I would go home and tell my mother about this, and she would hush me up and tell me not to dare let my father hear this talk. My father, brought up Southern Baptist, had studied Catechism when I started Catholic school, but he could never agree with the teachings. (I really wish that I could speak with him now as an adult about what teachings he didn't agree with, but he passed in 1981 at the age of 56.) Although Catholics are more tolerable of otherworldly beings, Baptists refer to this as devil worship and will have no part in it.

I learned that there was an angry God watching us, and the sentence of eternal damnation in the fires of Hell hung over my head always. I was a very shy child in school, and rarely asked any questions. But I remember in fourth grade raising my hand and asking the teacher a question that I really wondered about:

> *If the people in Africa had never heard of the God we were being taught to worship, when they died, were they going to Hell?*

The teacher asked me what *I* thought. I answered that I didn't know (this is why I was brave enough to ask her). She said, very confidently, *"Yes, they would go to Hell."* I think this was an awakening for me. I just could not wrap my mind around that concept. That answer still bothers me to this day.

The next year, due to financial reasons, I was sent to public school. By this time I had two younger sisters. Interestingly, my sisters were only given a minimal bit of religious instruction. I can only surmise that it is because I am on such a spiritual journey that I had to experience all of that. During this time, my mother decided we would all go as a family to a Baptist church, just so it would seem we were all worshiping together. The Baptist church was so different! People were very friendly! (In the Catholic church, everyone at that time kept to themselves and Mass was very serious.) We joined the choir, went to Sunday School and tithed.

Everyone was white, except for one man who was of Jewish descent. However, not having felt different in the past, I didn't notice it now. The sermons were always delivered in a profound way. The pastor and his family seemed very nice. We went there a few years, and then it seemed we drifted away. In high school, I was no longer made to attend services, and my mother said in her heart she'd always be Catholic.

Fast forward a few years – I got married at 19 and my new husband and I moved west to the central valley of northern California. I gave birth to our first son the following year.

What a culture shock this move was! Our neighbors were white and Mexican. In my head, I knew that the Mexican people were "my people," yet they were so different from me - I felt no connection to them, even though I spoke their language. All of my life experiences were different, how I was raised was different, our outlooks on life differed. I couldn't relate, and that confused me. My move to California also put me in touch with my mother's relatives – aunts, uncles, cousins. But again, I did not feel open arms to welcome me. I was different. I had a white daddy. White man was the enemy in this new circle I was in. I was very hurt. My father's family in Mississippi and Louisiana always showed us great affection and made us very welcome. I felt I belonged. My paternal grandmother, who was Irish, was charming and full of love (a little too much – she married four times!). I KNEW she loved me.

My next door neighbor in the central valley was Jehovah's Witness. I had never heard of that religion at all. She had a young family and was very nice. She asked me to "study" with her. I didn't really know what that meant, but I agreed. I felt that I needed to provide some religious teachings for my child. At 26, I had my second son and by then had joined the congregation. At that young age, I felt that all religion taught "good". I wasn't aware of the underbelly of organized religions at that point. I worshiped there for two years, then I just fell away. Surprisingly, no one came to ask why.

The next decade was spent raising my family, working, relocating to the San Francisco Bay Area. A twinge of awakening began in my bones in my late 30s - a *whisper* to begin my spiritual search anew. I began with a class at a local New Age store in the Bay Area. The class was an introduction to witchcraft and the elements. I had no idea what I would be learning but I followed my intuition and signed up. This class led to many more classes, groups, circles, rituals and solitary work. At this point I also began a deep interest in the Tarot.

One of the things that I had to confront during this period of learning and searching was the fact that I didn't feel connected to the cultural or religious traditions of the families from which I was raised. I studied many belief systems and traditions. Some felt familiar, from others I felt aversion. I longed to find where I "belonged". It didn't seem to be in the Mexican traditions nor the Celtic. Yet I was always accepted and made to feel welcome in all of the groups and circles which I attended. It was ME who wasn't connecting with THEM on some level.

I meditated on this situation and pondered it for a long time. Finally, I realized there was a THIRD blood that ran through my veins – *the blood of the land of my birth*! This was a living thing – a tradition that was alive and awakening in me. Traditions were brought to Louisiana by the slaves taken from the Mother Land, Africa, and melded with the traditions of the original inhabitants, the Native peoples. Louisiana became a magickal gumbo – a bit of magick brought by the French, Spanish, Italian, African, Irish, German. The pot was stirred over and over until it became its unique flavor. I was not of a tradition of my mother nor my father – *I was of a tradition of the land of my birth!!*

The spirit of Marie Laveau began to speak to me, whispering to me as a mother would to a daughter. I became obsessed with her legend and read everything I could on her. I realized that Marie Laveau was my *spiritual mother*. She, also of mixed blood (black, Native American and French), walked the same streets as I walked growing up. She, too, walked through the park in front of St. Louis Cathedral, where I played as a child. The river that flows through New Orleans nourished her with its energy as it does me to this day. I began to feel that I did, in fact, have a tradition, a place and people to which I belonged. I had searched through the world's traditions and found that the answer was at the spot where I began, in my own land. Nothing more, nothing less. The spirit of the land, the river, the humid air, the food, music, humor – and most of all, the people of Louisiana – these are my people, they are my tradition. This is where I feel I belong.

Louisiana's magick is neither black nor white, but a blend. I felt that some traditions were too focused on "love and light and positive energy", whereas others go to the other extreme, using dark powers to achieve one's purpose or ignoring ethics. My tradition recognizes that there is a place for all of these energies and powers. It's in the mixture.

Now that I have found my place in this spiritual world, I decided to honor Marie Laveau by having her image tattooed on my calf, as well as her veve (symbol). I now walk proudly with her every day. The second part of my life will be dedicated to exploring magick and ritual as she did, as well as helping others find *their* personal paths.

Ayaba Nukua

La Pixie (Sandra Posadas)

This solitary guardian
belongs to the world of the dead.
Dwelling in her mythocracy,
she moves in unlit spaces
where the mystic's balustrade leads to
the other side of nowhere.

Tonight she beckons me
for the primary role in her dance
of ancestral tableaus that trail back
through nude primeval sands,
to the African bush.

Movement is her homage
to the beauty of outer darkness.
The blackness is vacant no more.
The insurgent currents rise
with a dense, polyphonic fugue.
It escalates as ancient
drums palpitate the pulse of slumber.
The innumerable sashes of turbulence
in her voluminous skirts embrace
me with cold mortality.

She welcomes wandering bodies.
They crowd the space around
with elation and euphoria.
They've come home.
The residue of their tears
is acrid and harsh.
It dissolves in my nostrils
and stings my lungs.

Lighting strings across
the landscape of

my darkening pupils.
Tendrils spiral about
my arms and ankles
and heave me down
into a lair of shadows
Mamá Oya, **I am home.**

Heart of My Heart

Crystal Blanton

I have never concentrated on race and was raised in an area that was not prominently Black. This helped to shape the way I looked at the world and how I was able to build a feeling of togetherness with my community regardless of what race I was. Growing up I felt like it was so important to move away from the color lines that define people and move towards a common ground of experience, love and togetherness.

Moving into adulthood I came to realize that my race was not something to shy away from and it was actually an incredible marker of my ancestry and the struggles they went through. I started to look at my differences within my physical community of non-black people and wore my skin as a badge of honor that showed pride in who I am. This realization was a large one for me and helped to morph me into who I have become. Although my adult ideals of race did not change in many ways, the way I identified with my blackness did. I still believe in being able to let our humanity define us as people but now I believe that the color lines are a celebration of diversity and not of separation.

Although my experiences as an adult have helped me to understand that I cannot move away from color and how that is a great blessing to embrace who I am, it become a real source of confusion when I came to the realization that I was going to be raising a child. My son is of mixed race; half White and half Black. He is a sweet blond haired, blue eyed, fair skin little boy who could easily pass for being White if it were not for some of his Black features. He has adopted my wide nose and large eyes, features I contribute to my Black heritage.

I look at my son and wonder what others will think about him and how he will be typecast into playing a role in society that is dictated by others expectations and limited judgments. Embracing my own fears while attempting to find a balance between who he is as a Black man or a White man is a challenge. When I consider our families spirituality and moving him more into a Pagan way of living, it feels like I might just be tipping the balance between the invisible line of his Black and White sides.

In my ideal world, my son would be able to embrace who he

is in all the many areas of his life and not feel like he has to choose or be placed in the position to figure out who he should be versus who he is. In a world that can often be harsh and lack empathy, I continue to fear that I will not have the right tools to help him integrate into society or our spiritual community. For a community that prides itself in a non-dogmatic sense of freedom, we carry a lot of prejudices of our own.

This thought leads me to thinking about how to create cultural diversity and sensitivity among those within the Pagan community. I do not feel that our community is based on segregation or prejudice, I actually feel quite positive about the Pagan community at large. However, I do recognize the huge disparities among the amount of different races in our community and how that might affect others of minority races from becoming actively involved with other Pagans. The more we are able to create a spiritual community that looks like the societies in which we live, the more we will be able to create a balance that shows the many different faces of the Gods to those around us.

How are we to show the children who are growing in a Pagan path that all people are the children of the Gods if we cannot show diversity in our spiritual community or in the faces of the Gods that we worship? This is something we see so often in Christianity; a white face that is Jesus. Growing up as a child I assumed that Jesus was White because of this very thing and today I understand how important it can be to see yourself in the face of God.

Black culture is one that is created by a mixture of things that lead back to the Americanized society in which we were integrated into. I have often found that much of African culture feels foreign to me and one that I cannot fully relate to. I understand that my long ago ancestors came from Africa but I have no direct connection to the customs of those times and much of what is taught to Black children comes from the culture we created, by default, after coming to America. In my opinion, this is often quite confusing in the process of figuring out who we are as a race, and has actively created an inner turmoil that manifests to a lack of pride and understanding. I feel this is often one of the reasons Black people are quick to absorb the cultures of others around them, because by default that is what we have been conditioned to do in order to adapt and survive.

When a minority chooses the path of being a Pagan this is often what we see happening and what I also experienced in my own life when I found my spiritual path. Although this can be a great process to be a part of, it can create another divide inside of a person that is already so culturally split. Walking the line between multiple racial cultures, and then incorporating a spiritual culture such as Paganism, is something that minority races must do a lot. Our history shows that Black people are good at keeping this balance and we are able to walk that fine line but history also shows that it is hard not to replace where we came from with who we are learning to become.

It is important to truly understand that the history of the transformation from Africans, to slaves, to citizens or African Americans and then to Black people includes a lot of generational brainwashing, confusion and dissociation from culture or true racial foundation. The Merriam-Webster Dictionary defines dissociation as "the separation of whole segments of the personality (as in multiple personality disorder) or of discrete mental processes (as in the schizophrenias) from the mainstream of consciousness or of behavior". The overwhelming correlation behind the psychological aspect of dissociation and that of the plight of the integration of Black people into the mainstream White culture is astounding.

As we are now at a place in our development as a religion to raise children in Pagan spirituality, this is something minority parents must keep in mind since much of Pagan culture is not the same as ours. Once again we are transitioning into a place where there is less representation of Black people and more emphasis on those of White decent. Not only is there a disproportionate amount of Blacks, there are a disproportionate amount of all minority races within Paganism.

This is one issue that is not always something to consider when Blacks are living on the Christian side of life. Since Christianity has so many different sects of worship and is not based mostly in European concepts, it is easier to find churches that have all types of different people there. Christianity does have that one common image of Jesus as a white man but the bibles description of Jesus (different from the widely known image) has served as a comfort to many Black people who are followers of this path. I wish we had something similar.

And like with Americanized Black culture, I have found that Black Pagans often integrate many different things into their spirituality to create something that fits and feels more comfortable. We see this from the slaves using Christian Saints as covers for their homeland practice, to Black Wiccans today who use African or Egyptian Gods in Wiccan circles. Eclecticism is how we were trained to survive in this country and something that has been engraved in the psyche of minorities as one of the most important survival techniques to have. How do I support a child in developing this skill spiritually? Again, these types of questions around raising children in Paganism that will continue to come up as more children come into this culture and have differing cultures of heritage.

I feel it is important to teach my son all the various parts of who he is and support an understanding of how that all comes together to make him a very special person with a very important path. It is important to teach him of all the Gods, from the Celts to the Africans, so he can see diversity in his beliefs while he is developing how it applies to him. It is important to explain the variety of ways that different altars might look and make the connection of why mommies looks like a combination of a Wiccan and Voodoo altar all together. I want to help him understand that spirituality is not cookie cutter and one size fits all; it is about comfort and being able to relate. And finally, I think it is important to help him understand that he is more powerful because he is a true combination of many different paths that all connect at the middle, all parts are just as important as the other and being Black is just as important as being Pagan.

While we move into the next generations of Pagans, it is good to understand how important it can be to make it as comfortable of an environment as possible to everyone who is called to walk the path of the Gods. I hope that my face is one of the many that creates a safe place of acceptance to others who are looking for a place to feel connection and spirituality among the Pagan community for his or herself and for the child that may be walking beside them. Today my son's altar is in his room with pictures of his ancestors, Egyptian statues, a Yemaya candle, a dragon, crystals, a Thor's hammer, dream-catcher and Bakugan cards on it. It is perfectly balanced for a multi-racial Pagan child who is learning to honor all parts of his being.

Affirmations for the multi-racial Pagan:

Children:
Walking the lines of different worlds,
Knowledge in my body works together in a beautiful swirl.
With the blood of my ancestors I feel whole,
Many stories of family I am told.
The Gods guide me on my path this day,

All confusion and doubt to go away.
Blessed Be

Adult:
White, Black, Diamond and Gold
Weave work of ancestry foretold
In honor of many I walk
With the voices of sacred talk
Illuminating path before me be seen
In the glow of divinity may I beam.
For this day I am within my power complete
And in front of the Gods I kneel before their feet.

Why Don't You Like Me?

Olivia Haynes

Being Black and Pagan is already difficult but to be Black, Pagan and wanting to date? That's a multiplex issue in itself. The problems for Black Pagans that want to date stem from mostly religious and fairly racial grounds. Many people are still fairly ignorant about Paganism, Witchcraft and Wicca and will believe that anyone who claims to be a Witch, Pagan or Wiccan is possibly crazy or going to cast a hex around breakup time. The racial issues that tie into the religious issues creates almost the perfect storm in that Blacks are assumed to be Christian (or possibly Muslim), no alternative. Christianity is such a linchpin in the Black mindset, whatever is considered outside of the religion is considered to be an act of sheer blasphemy. Contrary to popular belief, the Black race is a very conservative race, the acceptance of something such as Paganism would come along very slowly. In addition, many Black Pagans are involved in alternative culture, where there is already a profound lack of Black faces and hence a smaller chance of potential Black-Black relationships.

Black Pagans already have it hard enough finding their place in Black culture and the Black community. Often we are misunderstood, ridiculed, ostracized and even called "White" or "oreo" (Black on the outside, White on the inside for those not savvy with snack food slurs) because we don't practice Christianity. Usually when I mention that I'm Pagan (or God/dess forbid, I tell them I'm a Witch), I can bet a good sum that I will be asked within ten minutes or less if I am a devil-worshiper and despite even my best explanations, word will spread like wildfire that a Satanist is in the midst. This is not to say that Black Christianity is not charming. There are definitely some very beautiful aspects to the interpretation of the religion but Black Christians tend to be pretty good at foaming at the mouth when met with something radically different from what they were raised and told.

I'll be told about Jesus (despite being a young adult, Black, living in America and not under a rock) and if I know what I'm doing is a sin. I'll be asked a million and ten questions about the Bible and explain a million and ten times that Paganism is not a denomination of Christianity so stop asking me the same freaking question just worded differently a million and ten times, I'm not Christian. Not all Black Christians go into freak-out mode when they meet someone who doesn't hail a cross but they're not really the norm. For now, there really isn't any room for Black Pagans and whatever room we do have to express our opinions and faith is incredibly limited within Black culture and we're barely a blip in the Black mindset, we are the "other". If this is the Black perception overall, imagine the chance of having a normal Black-Black relationship.

I don't have a rolodex of relationships to speak of, for I'm not really the dating sort. Relationships do interest me but not strongly enough to waste incredible amounts of time and energy on something that isn't promised and doesn't often work out. Instead, I have my own one guy who I have dated and sadly broken up with over the summer after a long term relationship. He wasn't Black, he was Indonesian, Muslim and into the punk scene. Was he perfect in acceptance towards me being Pagan? He had some rough edges but that's a lot better than believing I'd hex him if he forgot my birthday. He knew about my religion – I make it a point to get that out of the way first so any reactions, whether good or bad, can be had and I get a glimpse of what my future will be like. He was a lenient Muslim himself but our religious views didn't really enter the relationship much, we were just another pair trying to figure out how to manage a relationship just like anyone else. What killed the relationship were communication issues but he was by far the most accepting guy (who was dateable) of my religion. It's probably going to be a long time before I find someone like that again and a longer time if I want the guy to be Black.

Most Black men I come across are Christian. I have only come across a very small handful of Black Pagan men and they're my friends, un-dateable or already in relationships. Even if I did meet a Black Pagan guy, it's not a promise that our individual faiths will mesh well enough for a relationship, as not all Pagans are alike. To have a friendship despite our differences is one thing, but a relationship with so many disparities is another. A lot of Black guys already have very odd and perplexing views about Black women and vice versa which make it difficult to date inside the race but to layer "I'm a Witch!" on top of that, I can probably be assured even if I lowered my standards to a blade of grass I wouldn't get much of a catch. (Well, I wouldn't have much of a catch with low standards anyways.) The responses I often get towards my religion are rather disheartening, no matter when I spill the beans about my religion. They tell me they worry I'm cutting off goats' heads or that I'm crazy because I believe in spells. (How odd, they believe in prayer, practically the same thing.) I get the "You're a nice girl and all but...." even from the nicest guys. I already have very discerning taste in men (must be intellectual, eccentric (but not psychotic), interesting, respectful, generous, non-egotistical, open-minded etc etc) so my pool is small enough but to be Pagan, it's like the pool turns into a drop.

Away from religion for a moment, there is quite a silent crisis in the Black perception of the opposite sex. Namely, we're taught to hate each other. Black women are taught that all Black men are sex-driven dogs with a remarkable penchant for violence. Black men are taught that all Black women are money-sucking harpies with a remarkable penchant for violence. This is a very small nutshell of a very big problem but the symbolism runs rampant in Black culture consistently from movies to music to simply how we treat each other. Black culture still has a sense of inferiority instilled from systematic psychological destruction of the Black mind during slavery times so when we're told that the Black wo/man is worthless, we're taught by society that a White wo/man is a greater prize instead. Even if the notion does not appear to be incredibly prevalent amongst Black women, it is with Black men seemingly. To have a White woman or even Asian woman is preferable than a Black woman because it is believed a White or Asian woman is more submissive and manageable, which harkens back to the idea of the Black harpy who swivels her head snakelike in consistent disapproval but also other very long ingrained racial gender stereotypes that pervade mainstream culture like a sickness. In Black culture, it seems to be more acceptable for Black men to date and mess about outside of race but if a Black woman does it, she's a deemed a traitor because "she holds the future of the Black race." I hear this saying all too often and find it to be complete and utter crap since Black women aren't Virgin Marys. There is no such thing as "the future of the Black race" with only half the equation. To penalize one side means to penalize the other, not ignore it, regardless of who is the guilty party. Even with or without the Black wo/man end of the equation, there can't be a Black relationship if one side is absent for whatever reason.

I have dated outside my race because I don't entirely care much about skin color as I do about treatment. I'm putting myself out there but my top preference is Black or Asian/American (to note the difference between Asian and Asian-American in one term) because I gel best with both cultures. If I meet a nice Asian/American guy who doesn't mind my religion and is fairly decent himself, I will date him. If I meet a nice Black guy who doesn't mind my religion and is fairly decent himself, I will date him. This probably won't increase my boyfriend pool much either way because of religion and the social stigma of the Black woman as well as interracial dating complexities but I feel if a person wants to date outside of race, that's perfectly fine, who am I to harp? However, the problems begin when the main reason dating inter-racially is because the person believes some ill-conceived notion that their own race is worthless.

Returning to religion, Black Pagans are held back further in dating than their White Pagan counterparts because of the smaller pool and added racial stigma. To date within race is to dredge incredible amounts of questions about devil-worshiping and "voodoo doing" as well as assumptions of attempting to be White since it would be considered absurd to be Black and not Christian (or even Muslim). To date outside of race is to be greeted unknowingly with unwarranted racist questions that no sound-minded Black person would want to deal with. In addition, immediate assumptions (and possibly overly patronizing praise) of doing voodoo or Egyptian work may also be made. There are many issues regarding dating out of race but one pervasive issue stems in-race and it is the accusations of being a racial "traitor" by other Blacks, regardless of gender.

I would love to have a nice sizable pool of guys to choose from, eccentric, lovely, smart, respectful, creative men. I also would like to not be judged by the simple fact that, yes, I do cast spells, no, I don't go to church and I sincerely doubt I'll be coming back to Christianity, and yes, I truly do promise not to curse your whole family line if you forget to get me a present for Valentine's, honest. I'm more of the "talk it out" sort and when I say "talk", I mean "discuss what went wrong and listen to both sides equally" not "scream at you for three hours straight" since that doesn't solve anything. I want to have a nice, normal relationship with a guy, no worries about whether he's making Wizard of Oz or voodoo jokes behind my back and I don't have to teach him practically from scratch about my religion...or he's willing to do some of the leg work about it.

Relationships are a lot of work and plenty of give and take as it is the union between two very imperfect individuals who come with their own perks, quirks, dreams and misgivings. Regardless of religion or race, this is any relationship. No relationship is perfect because no one is perfect and Pagans are no different. I know for fact I wouldn't want to be seen only as Witch because that's not all that I am, just like any other Black Pagan. We wanna date, love and get married too, just like everyone else.

Message from the Dark Goddess

Rev. Anniitra Ravenmoon

"Hear me and know me"!

SHE IS.......................

Out of the Black void came SHE! A CRY IN THE WOMB! OUR PRIMORDIAL BLACK MOTHER

QUEEN GODDESS IS ABOUT TO GIVE BIRTH!! UHMMMM UHMMMMM Her `Black void womb holds many secrets and revelations; She holds the act of regeneration. SHE KNOWS! WE

ARE THE FISHES! WE ARE CRADLED IN THE WARMTH OF HER BLACK WOMB!

MESSAGE FROM THE DARK GODDESS
"Hear me and Know Me! Here me and Know me, For I am your darkness! I am your inner self that is hidden and concealed! I am the part of you that you shield, cloak, guard, seclude, and cover! There are states of your inner being that you should release from your darkness: That you should send; "Out of the Darkness, and Into the Light!" Out of the darkness and Into the Light!" As you transition into the new wheel, you must "loosen, and release your negative aspects that you have been harboring and shielding, loose and release your hindrances, fears, oppressions,

Intolerances, hurts, sadness, anger!!! Send them "Out"!

Out of the darkness and into the light" Embrace Me! Your Darkness, and release your hindrances from me, your darkness, go into the light for healing and renewed energy, and go with blessings from the Dark Goddesses. "So Mote it Be" - Rev. Ravenmoon

Alafia, Hetep Pu:

My Name is Anniitra MaKafia UtchatiNu Ravenmoon, and I am writing a few words to describe my relations with the Goddess world from the perspective of a "Nubian Queen".

From the time that I embraced Goddess spirituality as my

own, late 80's - early 90's, I knew that I was stepping into a world of wonder; of coming "home". I had guardians at that time but did not know it. I was in my own party world so I had some acute awakenings by our "Mother" before I discovered there was a "Goddess World" out there!

I had searched within the Christian communities for a church to belong to, a church that made me feel good, a church that I could learn "the word" from. I enjoyed the services but didn't get the satisfaction that I was seeking. I would know when I felt it. I hadn't felt it yet. I would listen to the Male Pastors/Preachers on TV on Sunday.

To me it seemed they were always telling the womin in the church what to do! They seemed to ALWAYS be chastising the womin!!

And the church would be FULL of womin! I would get very angry. I would say to myself "is the Pastor down on the womin?? Why is he saying negative things and making the womin feel bad?? And why are they saying amen to that"?? (more on that later).

I would say to myself: "Why doesn't he just go on and read the Bible, not talk about the womin."

Maybe I would catch the service at a time when the Pastors had a message to give to the womin, but to me it always seemed as if the Pastor was instructing them on what to do, how to act, chewing them out or what not to do. I don't know, maybe I had a chip on my shoulder about Pastors putting womin down. Somehow, I knew that the Christian path was not mine.

I was saying to myself, *"when did the roles change so drastically? Why is it that every time I go to church, the Pastor is blaming the womin for something??"*

I knew there were great womin out there. To me the goddesses were, at first, a curiosity but I had the hunger to learn more, especially of our Black Mother

Rituals and Honorings

Even when I was in my living room performing my rituals, the drum was ever so prevalent. When I would attend the Pagan rituals it would mostly be celebrations of Greek Goddesses, the Greek Aspect of the Egyptian Goddesses, then Roman Goddesses. I honored them also but knew that they were not the first, that they came later on in our "Herstory". It was a huge learning process for me. I was fascinated with them. It was something about each of my

Goddess Guides that I saw in my early life.

I felt that my messages took me to them;. Kali-Sekmet-Morrigan-Oya, and Yemaya/Yemoja. I used to watch the faces of people when I told them I had Kali as my guide. They seemed to fear them, especially Kali and Oya. I didn't know that much about Kali either, I just knew that she was the first one in my life and had been for a long time. Oya and the others came later. Kali, and Oya are depicted as destructive goddesses but once you get to know them and work with them they are very proactive.

I usually was the only Black womin or you could count on one hand anyone as dark as me. It never bothered me at all. I already knew that we ALL come from her source in Africa and we ALL are from the Great Black Mother, so *"I walk with the knowledge of who I am"*

I would partake in any ritual honoring the goddesses and it didn't matter to me because I knew what the first mother was to any goddess that we honor today and that is our Black Mother . I was the only Black womin in my beginning and advance Wicca, and spellcasting class in 2000. I would see very few, if any, black people at some of the Fairs, gatherings, conferences, womins circles or other events.

Although I have seen a change in the last few years, I think there *should* be more womin of color, especially Black, embracing goddess spirituality.

There is a lot of fear out there among my people about goddess spirituality and especially honoring a womin as deity; even though in Africa that is how and where it started. Some of my people blame Eve for all of the wrongs in the world.

Western traditions of organized religions took hold of my ancestors who were brought over here in slave ships and the hold is very strong today, especially in womin of color. Even as we look around today we see how much womin still have to fight. Yes, I said fight!

Of course there is prejudice, on both sides.

The Black Goddess was first, SHE is our mother!   ALL Goddess womin know that.

Some of my European goddess colleagues accept that and some don't. Some admit this but don't care to acknowledge any further than that. *Some of them choose to work with and honor,* Greek, Celtic, Roman, and Nordic goddesses, and those goddesses ONLY. Then, I have other European goddess colleagues that honor, and include our Black Mother.

Some of my African goddess colleagues, by the same token, don't want to acknowledge none other than the African/Egyptian Queen/ goddesses.

To some, even the name goddess is too Western for them. Also, some wish to be non-inclusive of the European goddess womin. Then there are some black womin who fiercely guard their Christianity. I was on a black radio station a year ago, whereas the topic was different types of spirituality. One of the callers was a womin, who got the mic, and ranted about how she didn't want to hear that $%@@ and that Jesus was the King. I say that to say this, on both sides there are fierce disbelievers.

I have been asked by African womin why I embrace a European Spirituality. My answer was and is because all spirituality started in Africa. European spirituality has later beginnings. Black/African culture goes back thousands of years. We are ALL a part of a Whole! We, together, are a full Circle. Our Black mother is the beginning of our circle.

I am universal, knowing my lineage! Our Mothers picked ME! And I love them all. I believe in order to complete our universal circle WE ALL must mix and blend and Acknowledge our BLACK MOTHER!

Whether we want to admit it or not, our Black Mother was ALL of our becoming! The Greeks, Romans, Teutonics, Celtics were later.

I use different types of rituals from ALL goddess cultures, with Orisha being the root, and I like to construct my own. When I do that I mix and blend like a great pot of soup!

I am a Warrior Goddess for justice and truth. I am of a lineage of the Amazons of Africa. How do I know? I feel it. I love "high/spirited ritual", I love the drum call from the womb. A drum beat reminds me of our ancient ones and how they communicated. The African drums take us back to primal times.

I have always used the Orisha in my work, even before I was fully dedicated to them, and even though I only knew very little about them. Drumming, dancing and the honoring of the ancestors transcends time. We Homo sapiens come from that.

Ancient lineage whereas our ancestors were honored. Things my mama would do used to seem strange to me when I was young. Only when I started learning more about our Feminine Divine did I come to understand what I was seeing. I have learned more and am still learning more than I ever have in school about my African Heritage since being embraced by "SHE"! I would leave offerings at the dinner table, give a morning prayer and an evening prayer. When I was younger I did not know much of African spiritually. It was not spoken of in my home. It wasn't spoken even in school, only that we black people were probably from a lineage of slaves exported from Africa.

I have made it work for me. For deep within myself, I walk in the knowledge, that We All are from the primal Black Void "SHE" our Black First Mother.

My Opinion III

In the end it won't matter, we will ALL go back to our Source; 'SHE". Being a Nubian, Black Queen. I'll go anywhere, and represent our BLACK MOTHER EVEN IF I AM THE ONLY ONE THERE!

I continuously lead by example that *I am SHE: and SHE Is Me!.*

Those Goddess womin out there, be they white, red, yellow, brown, or black, can't complete the circle of life unless they include honoring our "Black Mother". SHE IS THE SOURCE!

We, as Black goddess womin, have to get out and represent! Not just stay in our own little huddles or cliques. Only if we are universal and our Black Mother is properly represented, no matter which group or coven we belong to, our circle will never be complete. You can't ignore or throw our Great Black Mother out! *We, as black goddess womin, can't look to anyone else to put her there but ourselves!* Our European colleagues ARE going to put the European goddesses out there for recognition, they already have. That is a good thing. We must do the same, just like most of your belly dances are from North Africa but you wouldn't think it. Black womin have to embrace that also, but that is another story.

"Speak their Names, for they still Live!"

Being Black and Pagan

K.W.

Being Black and Pagan isn't much different from being any other race and Pagan in theory. I worship some of the same Gods, I have an incense collection that is slowly taking over my house, and I celebrate the seasonal Sabbats with the same abandon as others do. There are differences, though -- however minimal -- and I think they are worth taking a closer look at. Please keep in mind that this is just my experience; I'm sure that it's different for others.

As a minority in a minority religion, the most frequently asked question I get is "How can you be a Pagan, you're BLACK!" This implies that my religion is defined by my race, an assumption that I hope no one thinks is valid. While it is true that the vast majority of African-Americans are Christian, there are those of us who walk a different path. This reaction of shock seems to come more often than from fellow blacks. There seems to be a stigma in the African American community towards anyone who is not the accepted norm. It most often rears its head toward homosexuals but anyone who has not conformed is looked upon with ridicule, distrust and to a lesser degree, pity. This is one of the reasons why I feel there are very few "out" minority Pagans. Another reason is some of the reactions we get from Caucasian Pagans. I doubt that most people even realize that they do it (I like to think that folks are a bit more enlightened now than in the 1950s) but there are reactions that I've grown to notice. The double takes I have gotten when I've entered a festival or the assumption that I'm just there to "look at the freaks". Well, it's made me uneasy and mostly unwilling to seek out other like-minded people. If someone treats me as "other" because of the color of my skin in a non-religious context, I can ignore it. I can be sad that they haven't gotten past that barrier and move on with my life, surrounding myself with people who do see past it. When it comes to spiritual matters, it's different. Religion is such a personal thing and while being solitary works for many people (and indeed, it has mostly worked for me) there is something empowering and wonderful about sharing an experience with other people. I liken it to going to a Daft Punk concert: pretty cool by yourself, mind-blowingly amazing when you have a couple hundred other sweaty bodies singing along with "Harder, Better,

Faster, Stronger."

Another assumption made is that if I am Pagan, then I must practice Vodoun and/or be pledged to the Orishas. If I am neither, then I must not respect my ancestors. This argument more than any other frustrates me. It assumes that you can tell my racial makeup by the color of my skin, it assumes that I'm ashamed to be an African- American, and it assumes I have no honor whatsoever for the family that bore me. None of these are true. A person is Called into service by the Gods in my opinion, and you have no control over Who it might be or what you are drawn to. I've found that this particular argument goes both ways, as I have seen my white friends who follow the path of the Orishas disrespected for not "following their own people." I believe some of this comes from the fear of cultural appropriation. While I believe that this is something we have to look out for, to blindly dismiss anyone who works in a tradition outside their racial makeup is foolhardy. If more people took the time to actually discuss matters rather than just assuming the worst I think it would do a lot to foster not only mutual respect, but understanding.

Some may be wondering if I have encountered any specific racism in my various travels as a Black Pagan. The answer is not as nearly cut and dry as I would like it to be. Blatant hardcore racism? No, not at all; if anything the comments I've run into more fall under the term "hipster racism" than anything else. I will say, however, that in my non-spiritual life I have rarely had any encounters with racism (a blessing), but I have had far more online and IN Pagan communities. The internet allows some anonymity in regards to race, but in face to face meetings this safety net of sorts is removed. I like to think that the comments are not made in true hatred, and truly I don't think they are. However, it is something I have to consistently worry about in my dealings with people. As a result I do very little networking with local Pagans, be it via our local Pagan pride days or frequent our local shops. While I realize this might be shooting myself in the foot as it were, the experiences I have had in the recent past have led me to this conclusion. I would love to be wrong, to be told that this really was something my brain has conjured up but I have seen the experiences of others mirror my own. I realize a lot of this is my conditioning as a black person. I almost always brace myself for backlash, especially when word gets out about the deities I worship. If I go into a certain situation expecting to be stared at, then on some level I'm going to get just that. If I pick up on those cues, then I think one of the most honorable things I can do is to teach others that the face of practicing pagans is always changing. I'm not going to lie, it's hard work (putting myself out there = AYIEEE!) but it's something I'm willing to try.

I believe that we need to realize that the faces of Paganism are constantly in flux. One shouldn't assume another's path or tradition by the color of their skin. We need to stop doing double takes when someone whom we think doesn't "look" Pagan shows up to circle, grove, or temple. If visible minorities within a minority religion are oppressed by their religious peers, how can the community grow positively and be healthy? I came to Paganism years ago because among other reasons it felt right. I believed (and still do) that one's race has nothing to do with how you worship. If I did, I probably would have never sought out Paganism to the degree that I have and my life would have been a lot less rich then it currently is. I certainly would have less incense that's for sure!

I would hate to think of the next generation of Pagans feeling unwelcome or scared for something they have no control over. There is far too much going on that threatens to tear our various sects asunder, let's not add to the pile with some pre-conceived notions of what a Pagan is "supposed" to look like. Race, Creed, whether you call quarters in a broomstick skirt or celebrate Deipnon in Dior, how you look should (to me anyway) have no bearing on how Pagan you may or may not be. My hope is that in the future there won't be a need for an article like this and that we as a religion won't bat an eyelash at minorities at our events. I'd love to be able to freely network face to face and swap thoughts/ideas as well as visit my local stores (one can never have too much incense) without the uncomfortable stares. I believe that there is a place for everyone in the myriad paths of Paganism.

Blessings to you and yours.

The Story of an African-American Priestess

High Priestess Lilith S.K.

During my 14 years of study in Witchcraft, Wicca, Shamanism and Paganism, I have found that Pagans of Color are hard to come by, or just simply in hiding. For years of my life I have searched far and wide to create a group based on African American, Neo Paganism and Wicca but to no avail; it's as if I am the only one who exists. While I know this isn't true, I often find myself wondering if the traditional stereotypes of our African American family culture and the binds that keep families of color separated from other belief systems are true.

Is it true that we must bind our beliefs solely within the Christian Hierarchy of religious followings? Do we tell our families that we hold a close belief in something other than the all-knowing, all-mighty God? How do we tell our families that we are not evil, and that we believe in the purity of nature?

Coming from a strict family of Deacons, Pastors and Reverends in the Christian Faith (not to mention the Catholics, and Jehovah's witnesses) didn't make my coming out so easy. When I was a young Pagan on my path to understanding the ways of the Goddess, I slowly came out to my family with little subtle hints that their way of religion was not particularly right for me and my spiritual tastes.

I would often deliberately sleep in on Sundays, ditch bible school, and refuse to sing in the choir- (er.. I mean I suddenly lost my voice, of course). I would spend many hours in silent meditation, out in public spaces (like the living room, or the front porch), which often lead to a lot of interesting questions. While this was probably not the best way to come out in a family so demanding of living a Christian life, it was a subtle way of letting them know that I had a different path to walk. Finally, I was kicked out of my mother's house for two different reasons. 1. For being a Lesbian Vegan (which lasted all of 2 weeks), and 2. For being a Witch (which apparently wasn't an "alternative phase" like my mother labeled it to be).

I remember my "awakening" to the old religion as clear as

114

day. I was in 8th grade at the time, and I had a vivid dream of Silver Spiraling Staircase. I can remember how brilliant it was, how intensely the stairs sparkled. As I walked up the stairs, I could hear a chanting, loud into the distance. When I reached the top of the stairway a door with bright Golden wings appeared before my eyes! With a child's curiosity, I opened the door, to see a Bright winged Mother watching me with a smile. Her crown so brilliant and her wings outspread so wide, she almost frightened me. I didn't run. I walked right in as the door shut behind me.

I woke up suddenly; gasping for air and sweating as if I had been running for miles. I couldn't forget that face. I couldn't forget those wings. I needed to know who she was. The very next day in school, my teacher slaps a book on each of our desks. It was some kind of book on Egyptian Mythology. I opened the book, and there she was. Isis was her name and from then on I began my search for her. I dedicated myself to her work. I became her child. And through the toughest times of my life, The Great Mother Aset (Isis) has walked me through my journey.

The very first book I had ever read was *True Magick* by Amber K. My mother actually found that book while "cleaning my room" and asked me if Christmas was out of the question. I started to explain to her the Pagan holidays, and what it means to be a witch- then she proceeded to tell my great-aunt, the devout Christian from Kansas and head of the family about me and my choice of religion. This caused an absolute riot in the family and I was thrown out immediately on the spot with no place to go. After a while of communicating with my mother and letting her read all the books I deliberately left laying around, she decided to let me back in the house if I promised to stop being a Lesbian, at least eat some chicken and not tell anyone about my choosing to be a witch. At least she let me have my spiritual choice; one down and one and a half to go.

I realized that it was the lack of education on Paganism that got me thrown out of my house. My mother commented on how my attitude had changed, and how I became a more peaceful person. She realized that I was not in a phase of rebellion against our families' religious choices. When she let me back in the house, I felt a sense of renewal and respect. I talked with my mother often, introducing her to the old religion and spending a lot of time educating her on the ways of the Craft.

After my mother and I settled our differences about the whole idea of me being a Pagan child, she allowed me to have friends of the same faith and decided that it was time for me to go and be myself. I knew that with all the knowledge I had taught her, this was not her path. While we bumped heads on beliefs, and could not connect with each other's opinions, it was then that she realized that I wasn't going to change my mind. In my mother's house it was difficult to become authentic to what I believed in. So with several events that lead me to believe my journey was elsewhere, I left, never to look back. I can't say that she ever really read any of the books I left for her, and I can't say that she ever understood what I believed in but through all of this I understood how lonely this path would be, and I was ready to accept that challenge.

At the age of sixteen I moved away to continue to lead a group or coven and study with only those that were serious about Wicca and Witchcraft. I refused to let anyone in our group unless they read at least 5 books pertaining to Witchcraft or Wicca and knew the basics of what our Spirituality was about. I look back know and realize that I have always been serious about my religion and have made sure that others around me radiated the same kind of energy that I did. I never let movies influence me and I never bothered to listen to what others said about me. I was once again the only African American of my group.

My group consisted of several different races and ethnicities- Puerto Rican, Vietnamese, Caucasian, Mexican and well me, the black girl and "High Priestess". I really hated the title of High Priestess because having read all the books that I took the time to read, I knew that there was no such thing as miraculously becoming a high priestess. I continued to soak in the knowledge of the Universe and made sure that our coven did what it had to in order to continue on its spiritual path. We were bound by the law of the Wiccan Rede and followed the Wheel of the Year. Sometimes I look back and think that I knew more than I do now and other times I wish that I could go back in time and teach what I know now at a more in depth level. Just like with any teenage years, some thought of Witchcraft as a phase and grew out of it, and some continued to believe and to seek out more of themselves within the hands of the Gods. I being one of them.

I believe in my faith, just like a Christian believes in theirs. I have values, morals, and look upon people with compassion. As a priestess of the Craft I have learned to embrace the cycles of life, death and rebirth; knowing that we as humans must return to the womb to be reborn again into another life. Paganism, in my eyes has been the only source of spirit that allowed me to connect with the feminine energies of the Goddess. It was my only source of love, abundance and understanding, and it has brought me nothing but wonderful bliss and has made my life truly centered and enlightened. I have to say that we all have our points where our lives seem tough but that balance is what makes us humbled within ourselves.

Although I am still looking for Pagans of color who have a sense of their own individuality and pride as Pagans, I am happy doing what I do best. I am now running a humanitarian business here in Portland Oregon that focuses on the Pagan community, I own an online Metaphysical Retail shop, a brick and mortar Pagan shop, teach workshops and classes in the Pagan community, Shamanic Soul coaching, Kundalini Reiki, Legal Rites of Passage, Public rituals and Journey work. I love having an open community center and know that the journey to my purpose has been found. As Pagan Clergy, I can honestly say that I serve the Goddess for a living. I've dedicated my life to healing and being a sacred mirror to those who need it the most. I am blessed in knowing that I am making a difference in people's lives and will continue to do so as a Priestess of the Old Religion.

-High Priestess Lilith S.K.

Neo-Paganism and My "Ethno" Struggles

Yvonne Nieves

I grew up in a Christian household. My father is an ordained United Methodist minister and my mother is a tenured English professor at a local college. Both parents have their Ph.D.'s and I have my own degrees in Anthropology and Sociology. Social work and community service has always been important to the people in my family, and I even took this to the next level by becoming an activist for human rights struggles in my community. I recently converted to Neo Paganism, and am out of the closet to most of my friends and family. You must know that my ethnic makeup is Puerto Rican and black (my biological father –whom I have never met- is African American) .

I wanted to write this piece as a commentary about some things that have been on my mind regarding the Pagan community. Let me explain this further. To begin, the community in which I was raised was comprised of Puerto Ricans and blacks in Chicago. The Puerto Ricans in my neighborhood are of the first, second, third, and now fourth generations (I am of the third) here in the United States. Growing up, anyone who practiced the Yoruba tradition of Santeria was often perceived in a negative light. I presently have friends that are sympathizing with the West African religion and are even incorporating it into their Christian beliefs. But I have not chosen that path. Or rather, that path has not chosen me. Let me break this down further for you.

The island of Puerto Rico, also known as Borinken, has been recognized the most important place in the world, and its importance is referenced in popular socio-political texts such as Reproducing Empire by Laura Briggs and Harvest of Empire by Juan González. And while I won't go into an explanation of the history of the country, or how it was colonized by Spain and then taken over by the United States in 1898 (fell free to do your own research on this) , it is important to know a little bit more about the bloodlines of the people in the Puerto Rican Diaspora.

The most noted indigenous people to inhabit Puerto Rico

were the Arawak and the Tainos (again, feel free to do more research on this topic) . Ponce de León, Spanish conquistador and first Governor of Puerto Rico appointed by the Spanish crown, led exterminations of thousands of indigenous people there in the early 1500's. By the mid 1700's, thousands of Africans had been brought over to Puerto Rico through the slave trade or emigrated from other parts of the Caribbean for work opportunities. At the same time, many other people came to Puerto Rico for a variety of reasons, including Arabs, Dutch, Irish, Italians, British, Chinese, and the list goes on. (I have two cousins with bright red hair –one is mulato with green eyes, the other with a European appearance with blue eyes- a true testament to our Northern European roots.) My family, like most other immigrant families, came to the States during the 1950's for economic reasons, and stayed.

Fast forward thirty years and you have me, a descendant of the indigenous people of the Caribbean, of West Africans slaves, and of European settlers. I've always been sympathetic to Wicca, however wouldn't dare hop over the besom to cross to the other side because there was no one else that I knew who was a Wiccan in my community, plus I was raised in a Christian household. A few months ago, a divine Yoruba deity came to me in a dream and spoke her name to me, which gave me the kick in butt that I needed to finally dedicate myself to the Goddess.

After I came out of the closet, a few of my friends in the community asked me why I am not practicing Santeria. I can only imagine that some extended cousins of mine who dance, sing, and drum bomba and plena (music-based art forms that were passed down by slaves in Puerto Rico) wonder to themselves what's going on with me. My aunt, who is exploring Palo Mayombe of the Bantu region, wants me to "go to [her] side." I simply have to politely say, "It's not necessarily my path."

Right now I am solitary, and meet the outside Pagan community with trepidation. I'm not sure that I will meet many other people of color like me, and am slightly concerned with having to confront racism in this religious community as I have everywhere else in my life. I am already being faced with the struggle of working as an 'undercover' Pagan at a program funded by the Catholic Church. I am being questioned by my Puerto Rican community for choosing a Eurocentric Pagan path (and sometimes it does go right over their heads, which is fine by me) , instead of an African religious tradition.

I do not doubt my path, or myself because at the end of the

day, I know what resonates true to me right now. I don't have much of an opinion about what others choose to practice, nor do I think they should have an opinion about what I practice. But let's be real. It's going to happen. And knowing that this will be one of my primary struggles along my path, I know that I can only be consistent, persistent, and continue on my own question for knowledge and truth within myself.

I do feel that much of the Pagan community can relate to my complex story (and it gets even more complex when I tell people that I'm a huge metal head) , but I do look forward to being pleasantly surprised by the greater Pagan community. I'm looking forward to feeling welcome in various circles and being an insider. I hope to network and help in any way I can, because of my personal mission of service. With a positive approach, a willingness to be open to new ideas, and an open heart, I know I'll come across the right people that will help guide me along my path.

Forgotten Lessons

Yonv Unega

There are many paths when it comes to spirituality. Some people find their way in the teachings of the bible or other religious literature; others find their path by looking within. So often we look to be lead down a path, like someone out there has a map and will lead us to the promise land. This is simply not true.

All we need is within us and throughout the centuries this knowledge has been lost. It has been washed from our subconscious mind and replaced by insecurity and fear.

Fear is used in a lot of religious text, from the bible to the Qur'an. Have you ever heard the phrase "a god fearing man"? A "God Fearing Man" is supposed to mean a good person. Personally, I fear man more than God for it is man that wages war behind the cloak of religion.

I am an individual made up of many different nationalities. Some of my family would tell me stories of my ancestors; Shaman, Druids and Christians, to name a few.

My grandfather was Irish and very Christian, so I was forced to go to church when I was young. While I was in church, as a child listing to the preacher address his "flock" and use fear as a tool to manipulate his followers into being good "sheep" or they'll go to hell, it would confuse me.

If God loves all of us except, gays and other non Christians, how is he a loving God and why am I scared. If we are made in his image, are we not gods and goddesses? Shouldn't we be looking towards being fearless?

I was lucky enough to have conversations around spirituality with my mother and my grandmother. It was those conversations about Mother Earth and Father Sky that felt true to me. My grandmother was Native American and my mother spoke of Druids. This affected me deeply. I would receive constrictive ideas around religion from my grandfather and open minded free thinking ideas from my mother and grandmother. This imposed an negative perception of Christianity upon me. As I grew older and I understood the bloodshed that occurred during the crusades and understood man's reasons behind religion, I could no longer considered myself a Christian.

I did not want to be associated with a practice claiming to praise a benevolent higher power but killing all of those who failed to follow suit.

My grandmother and mother both wanted me to be a free thinker and not swayed by the masses. My mother would say things like "your the master of your destiny" and she encouraged me to trust my insight. She would talk to me about my mind's eye and how to see truth. My mother spoke of karma and the rule of three. She talked of trees and how important they are to our survival.

Spending time with my grandmother in her garden felt like work when I was young, little did I know those conversations would be some of the threads that would tie together the feelings and ideas I hold to be true today.

My grandmother would speak of the circle of life and how no one or no thing was all good or all bad. She explained that there is an intricate balance in all things and that we, as people, have lost touch with this. She spoke of the Mother Earth and not wasting her gifts. She spoke of the Father Sky and how we are all connected.

As a husband, father and grandfather I see how important these conversations were in shaping how I look at the world and how we fit in it. I want my children to understand that they hold all of the answers and all they have to do is ask themselves the right questions. It has been a intense and necessary part of my personal spiritual journey to learn how to connect with the spirituality inside of me, like that of my ancestors, instead of looking outside of me for validation and understanding.

I have found that being of mixed culture comes with a higher responsibility to teach our children how to make these connections for themselves. One good way to coach children into being open minded is to have well timed conversations and ask open ended questions when possible. It could be very valuable to ask a child what their understanding of a higher power is? How does he or she think believing in a higher power can help him or her? What does being spiritual look like? Get kids involved with performing random acts of kindness and discuss with them how it felt. Continuing to have conversations, so they can choose a spiritual path that will help them grow, is essential.

I have learned that my experiences have helped to shaped my understanding of who I am spiritually and without those times of my life that forced me to reflect inwardly, I would not be the person I am. I have been disconnected from the culture of my ancestors because I was raised in a White world with the expectations of others but my native culture is not lost to me totally.

It doesn't matter how we get there, what matters is the lessons learned in our journey and how we apply those lessons to our life.

Pele in the Catholic Church

Leilani Birely

I always had a fire burning in my belly that kept me from fitting into molds that were too tight to contain my passion. I wasn't what you'd call a bad girl but I was definitely not the definition of what a 'sweet good girl' is either. Grandma Chong had her concerns with 'my mouth' as it was often put and I was often described as being 'sassy'. My sisters and I were raised differently than my mother was taught by her parents, Grandma and Grandpa Chong. One of the main differences is that she fostered an environment where we were allowed to speak our truth. She did not want us to follow her own upbringing of being raised with 'fear and an iron fist'. I remember growing up hearing stories about how my mom always had a vision for herself, as a young girl, that when she had kids she would make sure she raised them with more trust than she had. Her kids would be allowed to say what they had to say. I realize now what a truly valuable gift I was given in this.

I remember the time I refused to take Communion anymore in the Catholic Church when I was 14. We were in Hawaii for the summer visiting our grandparents, which was usually the case, and our routine was one of regular Sunday church services. Grandma Chong sang in the choir and Grandpa Chong collected the church monies in the long handles basket brought to each pew. I knew that they were both very devout Catholics and also prominent and dedicated members of Holy Trinity Catholic Church on O'ahu. I always felt like a visitor in someone else's faith during my years being raised in the Catholic religion. Most of what mass represented did not resonate with my soul's passion. I did like getting up and being able to move when communion was served but the dry Styrofoam like wafer that ended up sticking to the roof of my mouth was less than desirable. I never felt connected to eating the body of Jesus Christ, although I did appreciate the reverence I saw on the faces of the participants that accompanied this part of the ceremony.

After one too many sticky wafers in my mouth, I told my mom that I was finished with having communion; I didn't like the taste and didn't want to participate in this part of the ceremony any more. I remember my mom feeling that it was ok with her and being supportive of my choice but being concerned about what my

Grandma would think. Frankly, I really didn't care what Grandma would think as I didn't see the connection between what her thoughts and my desires were. After church one Sunday in the car, while we were waiting in the crowded line to exit the parking lot, I announced that I no longer wanted to take communion. My Grandparents horror was immediately apparent and I was greeted with angry tones and words that said, "how dare you refuse the Lord's body" and that it was a sin for me to "have such thoughts much less speak them aloud and act on them".

I knew that when my mom's new and improved style of child rearing and my grandparent's values locked horns, there was sure to be some heated words. I was adamant in my position. I was simply not going to budge or change my mind. My mom backed me up as she often would with her parents by saying, 'back off ma and daddy, these are my kids and I'm raising them the way I want to'. Her words were hot and her intention clear, they didn't fight back. I remember feeling a teenage satisfaction that an adult had sided with me and stood up to authority. I now know what an act of courage it was for my mom to stand in her truth, speak it and show me as a young girl what it was to stand up for what you believe in.

One of the things that I did adore from my Catholic upbringing was Mary reverence. I am still, to this day, an active devotee of Our Lady of Guadalupe, Tonantzin; Mary and all incarnations of Mary Mother of Mercy and Compassion. Grandma Chong and my mom both had elaborate home altars decorated with Mary statues and adorned with candles and flowers. I still have my mom's Mary statue and placed Her on my desk to help me with the writing and compassionate communication. I have made several pilgrimages to sacred sites where Mary is honored including Our Lady of Peace church in Santa Clara, CA where there is a 60 foot statue of Mary. During the month of May, Mary's month, there are dozens and dozens of buckets filled with flowers brought by those that have come to honor Her.

I took a group of women to the church grounds and we did ceremony there with an altar made of a Guadalupe blanket and many novenas with images of Mary on them. There is a walking rosary on the grounds of this church and many folks looked with curiosity as a circle of 8 women sat around an altar of Mary on the grounds of a Catholic Church.

At one point, a woman from the church approached us. A couple of the women in our group stood up as she asked us, 'are you devotees of Our Lady'. They reverently replied, 'oh yes'. She mentioned that they needed to be careful of 'circle groups'. As she walked away, we were all taken by how our pagan worship did have an overlapping piece. It felt risky in many ways to bring our Goddess worship to the church grounds but I know that we felt as much right to celebrate Our Lady as anyone else. Wherever She is worshiped is my altar.

She Came in a Dream

Yvonne Nieves

She came to me in a dream. The air felt dark and damp, and in a flash I saw her. She was all in white. The wind blew briskly from the west, her skirt flowed toward the east,. And with her hands sweeping the air in an upward motion, she spoke her name to me: "OYA!" She was gone as quickly as she came.

It was that very next morning that I knew my life would never be the same. I had heard voices before, non-threatening ones that would provide me with random information. My first experience with clairaudience came years before, when I heard a gentle voice say, "Janus plant." Unafraid, I psychically asked the voice to explain the statement. In return it said, "Injury sales. Many sales." I Googled the word "Janus" and found that Janus is a Roman god of beginnings and transitions. Sacred plant was mentioned throughout the Bible. I learned that the Janus plant is used as a key ingredient in sport medicine. This synchronicity allowed me to acknowledge my auditory gift. Knowing deep down that in time there would be more to this, I decided to simply accept the message and wait.

I instinctively called my aunt, who had been studying spiritism and asked her, "Who is Oya?" She said that Oya is an Orisha, the goddess of wind and a guardian of the cemetery gates. My aunt exclaimed, "Girl! She chose you!" I quickly scrabbled to my trusty and reliable Google again. "Who is Oya?" I kept asking myself as I typed in all of the related keywords that I could think of. "What does this all mean?"

Not much about Oya was available, only a few prayers and several repeating images. But nevertheless, those few photos resembled exactly who I saw in my dream. It was Oya and she had blessed me.

It was then that I ran into my first list of correspondences on the web. Oya has been associated with Kali, a Hindu deity, protector of children and "The Fierce Goddess." Years before I had felt a bond with a random picture that my tattoo artist had drawn up of Kali. Not knowing who she was, or what her name was, I opted to get a portrait of Kali permanently tattooed on my right arm. To make matters more interesting, the day I began my three-quarter length sleeve was Ash Wednesday.

Once I made the connection between Kali and Oya, my mind raced back to a dinner conversation I had with a close friend of mine who was about to make *santo* in Santeria just a year back. He told me to be careful, that my tattoo was now embedded in me and that I was a child of Oya. Of course I shrugged him off but deep down inside I knew that there was more to this.

But now I felt a conflict rise within me. Growing up in a Puerto Rican community in Chicago, people who practiced this religion were stigmatized. Even though just about every Puerto Rican family that I knew had a person who clandestinely practiced this mysterious form of spirit manipulation in a secret back room of their home, it was nothing to boast about. Santeros were the secret that each family held. They were the people who my grandmother went to when she wanted her cards read or for a special herbal concoction to heal our external, and sometimes even internal, wounds.

While Santeria was still a mystery to me, and in the deep-rooted layers of my being something taboo, I decided to construct an altar to honor the beautiful goddess in my dream. Even though I am the daughter of an ordained United Methodist minister, I had lived a secular life for approximately 13 years and collected random items from around the world while I studied Anthropology in college. On the altar I carefully laid out a couple of candles, a sage bundle and my favorite Nag Champa incense. I included several stones that I collected over the years, including a six-sided rose quartz pendulum that had been blessed at the Pyramid of the Sun in Teotihuacán, Mexico. One month later, on the great sabbat of Samhain, I dedicated myself to the Craft. To me this meant that I would be propelled on to the path of Spirit, and forward in the way of the Goddess.

Me deciding to practice 'The Craft' did not mean that I would convert to Wicca. The word itself did not resonate within me. I knew that in order to be Wiccan one would have to undergo a series of trainings and practice in very specific manners. I extensively researched the term, and found much information on the Internet about people claiming to be Wiccan. But Wicca felt cultish to me, exclusive, and extremely European. Like Santeria, Wicca was not for me either.

I went to my local library, and found three books that would shape my views on the topic of being a witch. The authors Raven Grimassi and Patricia Telesco gave me great and basic foundations on how to work with herbs and crystals, as well as explanations on the Wheel of the Year. I mostly related to Grimassi's stregheria (or Italian witchcraft) on a culturally symbiotic level. I truly felt a connection between the knowledge he shared in his book and my own Latino upbringing. The third author, Kate West, wrote about Wicca with such arrogance, that it turned me off to defining myself as a Wiccan.

The term "pagan" intrigued me more. I was familiar with the term because some of my favorite metal bands have been labeled with the sub-genre "Pagan Metal." Many of these bands have produced music with energetic and upbeat rhythmic undertones from northern Europe, while other pagan metal bands have darker, doom sounding tunes with lyrics about some of my favorite mythical characters like Odin and Thor. For many years, I had on the dance floor at local Latin rock shows in Chicago and danced round and round with my Mexican friends to *Fiesta Pagana* (or Pagan Festival) by Spain's premier pagan metal band named Mago de Oz (or Wizard of Oz). This tune always gets everyone revved up and we dance like our Irish ancestry is exploding through our arteries. Perhaps the excitement can be attributed to an alcohol induced trance. I digress.

I settled on defining myself as pagan. To me this meant that I could apply my ideas and beliefs, and whatever else came naturally, to my spiritual practice as I please. I would not have anyone telling me that I needed to select a practice based on my diverse cultural heritage; the Arawak, West African, and European within me. Being pagan meant that I could prominently display the pentagram in my home and place a replica of a Taino *cemi* on my prosperity altar full of Buddhas in the southeast corner of my home (based on Feng Shui principles). Paganism meant that I could listen to heavy metal, my music of preference, and still drum and dance to Afro-Puerto Rican *bomba* rhythms in remembrance of the slave struggle in Puerto Rico. Ultimately, paganism meant that I could be myself; the weirdest, most mysterious, on-the-fringe-of-society gal who alters rules to fit her needs and master the occult. Kind of like my matron deity herself, Oya.

Coming Into the Tradition

Uzuri Amini
(Ishe Fa'lona Oshun Iya Oshogbo)

As a Christian I experienced wonderous and miraculous things. Through my 10 year issue of faith I experienced wondrous and miraculous things. Now in The Tradition I have experienced wondrous and miraculous things. -Uzuri Amini

Many times I have talked about my move from Christianity into the Ifa spiritual tradition of the Yoruba people of West Africa. I have felt blessed that throughout my life Spirit was there for me, helping me to survive the challenges that life brings.

As a child I went to church on Sundays with my great aunts, my grandfather's sisters. Aunt Lu Emma was the elder sister who left the farm to go to school to be a teacher. After she left she slowly reached back and pulled her younger brothers and sister off the farm too.

Aunt Anita, who was the baby girl in the family, married a minister. In fact he was a Presiding Elder of the C.M.E. (Christian Methodist Episcopal) Conference in Arkansas.

Raised on a farm in the Searcy, Arkansas area, the Christian church was a cornerstone in their upbringing. They learned the tenets of the church and took all of their worries and concerns to "the Lord in prayer."

My mother worked on Sunday and would question me when she came home from work. "What did the minister talk about in church today? What did you learn? Do you have any questions?" Sometimes I did and sometimes I didn't. When I did my mother worked at answering my questions to help me have an understanding of what had been said.

The other religious element in my life was Catholicism. In order for their children to get a better education in the segregated south, many African American families sent their children to Catholic school. In order to attend these schools children had to review and learn the Catechism, plus be able to answer any one of the 100 questions in the back of that little blue book.

I remember my mother studying with me when she came

130

home from her day job working at some white family's home. Tired but determined that I was going to learn everything I had to know to get into this "better" school, she would repeatedly read the questions to me . She cheered when I was right and prodded me with hints when I was wrong. If that didn't work, eventually she told me the answer.

Sitting in front of Sister Superior, my mother was very proud of me when I answered all the questions correctly and was allowed to start school at the age of five.

A part of my school instruction was about Catholic doctrine and I dreamed of being confirmed. Every other Friday the entire school would attend mass but only the Catholic children could take communion. If I was Catholic I could join the long line of children standing at the altar with their small tongues out waiting for that little wafer. Oh how I envied them.

After we left Little Rock, Arkansas, when I was 8 years old, the Sunday questioning stopped. We were living in Seaside, California now and my mother had other things on her mind, from how to survive in this new environment living with her dad (my grandfather), to where could she find work or who would be a proper suitor for her. Those things took over her mind. Now Grandpa's brother, Uncle Thomas, was the pastor (another C.M.E.) of the church I attended on Sundays.

Catholicism became a consideration again in the 6th grade only because of my mother's friend and all of her family members who were Catholics. Mama thought it would be good for me be one too. Again I was on my way to that little white wafer. A date was set and I had my white confirmation dress. Once again I had passed all the prerequisite tests but two weeks before I could go through the ceremony we moved away to Missouri and finally back to Arkansas.

Once I returned to Arkansas my only foundation was the C.M.E. church. It sustained me as I went through marriage at 17, having children, and divorcing at twenty. I escaped a difficult, untenable, destructive union using Psalm 27:1 (King James Version) *The LORD is my light and my salvation; whom shall I fear? The LORD is the strength of my life; of whom shall I be afraid?* as a mantra.

From there I found myself questioning everything about life, living and love, as I struggled to raise my two children alone. I questioned authority on many levels as I sought to get some understanding of who I was and my purpose upon the earth. During this ten year period of my life, I only went to church for weddings and funerals as I held a belief that I didn't have to go to church every Sunday to have a relationship with God. If and when I needed to I could pray/talk to the Creator at any time; be it walking to work, as my children played in the park or before I went to sleep at night.

I moved with my children to California, where I discovered a new world in which to live my life. Finally, I escaped from my family who had both shaped who I was (this questioning human), and the ones who had held me back from finding out the things I really wanted to know about.

I continued to have my talks with the Creator, as I discovered that there were other spiritual disciplines to learn and explore. Buddhism and chanting was one. I took my children with me when I went to explore the ashram near where we lived. I thought it would be a good thing for all of us to learn how to meditate and be calmer through chanting. The quiet and the chanting proved to not be for us. For me it didn't fill that inner empty forever questing place, so I kept looking for other avenues for my spiritual needs to be fulfilled.

This new lifestyle also afforded me a chance to go to junior college where I was bombarded by more new people and ideas. There I met Luisah Teish after she performed a piece embodying the spirit of Sojourner Truth. After her inspiring performance I sought her out then and there. Thus began a friendship between two southern women dreaming about mutual aspirations of writing books, and traveling in the world.

Spending time with Teish was always an adventure whether we sat in her living room, were picnicking in her backyard under umbrellas or going to see some kind of performance. Being different and expansive, I took my time in asking her about the glasses of water on the table behind the sheer white curtains in her apartment. I don't remember what she told me at the time but now through my spiritual practice and experience, I know this space was in remembrance of her Ancestors.

One evening we went to a performance of drums, singing, and dancing that seemed to focus on some Afro-Caribbean myths. And so it went until, through time and change, we lost touch with each other.

After a few years, while Teish and I were absent from each other's lives, I began to study metaphysics. Dictionary.com defines metaphysics as "The branch of philosophy that deals with the first principles of things, including abstract concepts such as being, knowing, cause, identity, time, and space." For me I found metaphysics to be a study of the self on many levels.

My teacher, whom I will call Ms. Wisdom, taught me many things. Among them were - How to acknowledge and work with spirit guides, see and read auras, how to meditate, how to see beyond the mundane level of life to help others and about universal law. I began to know myself in ways that I hadn't ever considered while I delved into the inexplicable in life.

During this time I was able to do in-depth healing of some of the childhood trauma I had suffered. As a part of this Ms. Wisdom led me through a forgiveness ritual which helped me to let go and transform the old hurts and harm done to me as a child. These studies also buoyed my faith in the ability of one to grow and change, the strength of the unknown and the spiritual power that can be sourced in difficult times. I continued to learn things until life brought Teish and I together again.

During the intervening years Teish was growing too. She was initiated into the Lucumi spiritual tradition for Oshun, spirit of the sweet waters of the world who is the deity of love, art, sensuality, sexuality, fertility and creativity.

Attending a bembe (a celebration) after a mutual friend was initiated our paths crossed once more. Happy at seeing each other again we picked up our friendship as if we had only seen each other yesterday. We talked about what we had been doing and how we were growing.

It was at this event that I tripped over some kind of pot at the edge of the ceremonial area and immediately found Teish staring me in the eyes asking," when are you going to do this?" My reply was simple. "Never." How little I knew of what Spirit had planned for me.

Teish and I once again spent time together. Soon I felt myself being more and more interested in her spiritual practice. Besides my metaphysical studies I began going to ceremonies and rituals that Teish held. I found by participating in these rituals something stirred inside me that felt both ancient and genuine, as well as spiritually fulfilling.

I kept moving forward on this path until one day in my metaphysical session Ms. Wisdon said to me,

I see that you have walked down this one path and now you have come to a fork in the road. One road leads to the right, one road leads to the left and you must choose which one to continue on your journey. The only thing I can tell you to help you choose is that both paths lead to the light. Also there is this African man dancing behind you waiting for you to choose." As I drove to my first Ancestor ceremony at Teish's house I pondered what she had told me. I didn't know what my choice would be.

That night I participated in the Ancestor ceremony and observed first hand as Teish channeled the spirit of Freda, an escaped slave from the 19th century who survived in the Louisiana swamps for many years. I remember even now how the hairs on my arms stood up as I realized that this was no performance. This was real! I felt it from the inside out as I had arrived in the presence of the Ancestors.

This last experience touched me so deeply that I knew I had to be a part of this spiritual tradition. Thus I stepped forward to begin a new adventure in my life that would forever change me.

Years later I came to understand that the meeting of 3 roads is called a crossroad in Yorubaland. Eshu, in his many manifestations, is the "Keeper of the Crossroads and Divine Messenger." This is who Ms. Wisdom saw when she looked beyond me as I stood in the center of the crossroads.

I made my choice to go on this path. As I have traveled this path I have experienced healing over and over of my human maladies that many of us confront every day. It is a journey that through all the challenges I've encountered I've never regretted.

Libations for World Ancestors

Chief Luisah Teish

The Yoruba people of Southwest Nigeria say that "those who go before us make us what we are." The truth of this saying is evidenced in the history and the culture of the African American.

As proud African people, we Egyptian astronomers walked among the stars. The Dogon slid down to Earth, the Congolese danced with the wind and the trees, and the Masaai tamed the wild beasts. We organized ourselves into communities that invented writing and education was born. We discovered iron and forged the tools of Agriculture. With our surplus of the Earth's wealth we built the great and wealthy empires of Kush, Songhai, and Shona. We opened trade routes that reached across the Ancient World from the Mosque in Timbuktu to the Yellow River in China. An African Queen dressed herself up one day and changed the gold standard of the world.

We tempered bronze, wove cloth and extracted medicines from the leaves of plants. We shaped instruments from raw materials. Then we improvised on the movement of the bushcow, let our voices ring and created a myriad of ways to praise the Creator and the Creation.

When the invaders landed and dark days fell upon us, we endured the trauma of being ripped away from our beloved Mother Country. As we passed through the last door, stripped of our possessions but not our pride, we called out to Her in song.

We held our spirits safely in our breast and hummed our way across the watery abyss.

And on every shore where we landed our beauty created music and dance, our knowledge and skill created instruments and inventions; and our undying spirits gave birth to Spiritual traditions that have endured and flourished and populated our world.

Now we pour libations in honor of a partial list of the spiritual traditions celebrated by people of African descent worldwide.

Please feel free to pour water or wine on the Earth and call out the names of prophets and practices that you honor and bless. When pouring the libation we say "Mojuba O, Love and Respect to You."

1. To all the ancient ones whose names have not been remembered. Mojuba

2. To the traditions of Egypt, the Metu -Neter, the Fahamme

3. To Coptic Christianity

4.. To the Falashes, the Black Jews

5. The Akan of Ghana

6. The Yoruba of Nigeria

7. The Fon of Dahomey

8. Inkisi of the Congo

9. To the Shone and the Zulu of So. Africa

10. To the Macumba and Candomble of Brazil

11. To the Kumina and the Rastafarians of Jamaica

12. The Shango Baptist of Trinidad and Tobago

13. To the Lucumi and Santeria traditions of Cuba and Puerto Rico

14. To the Rada and Petro traditions of Haiti

15. To the works of Mam'zelle Marie LaVeau and Mother Catherine Seals of New Orleans

16. To Oyotunji Village in So. Carolina

17. To the Traditions of the people of the Gullah Islands off the Georgia Coast

18. To the Blackhawk traditions of African and Native Americans

19 To those who have embraced interfaith and world spirituality

20. To black Pagans Who revere the Earth

21.And to those yet unrevealed to us we say.

"Mojuba O, Love and Respect To You"

Chief Luisah Teish

Writers' Bios:

Crystal Blanton's book "Bridging the Gap; Working Within the Dynamics of Pagan Groups and Society" came out in 2010 and addresses ways that techniques can be used to support the growing dynamics within the Pagan community. Blanton is a High Priestess and ordained minister with Covenant of the Goddess, Rising Phoenix Tradition and Dance of the Spirit Moon Tradition and is a student mentor. Blanton is a trained and experienced Registered Addictions Specialist in the field of drug and alcohol counseling. She has worked in the field of counseling for the last 15 years, 11 of those have been within the drug and alcohol treatment field. She currently works with adolescent treatment of drugs and alcohol. She is a mother of four, grandmother of three and a married wife of fifteen years. Blanton has been published in Circle Magazine, The Belefire Magazine, Timeless Spirit Online Magazine, Witchvox and Pagan Pages. Blanton lives in the San Francisco Bay Area with her husband and children.

Luisha Teish is a writer, storyteller and creative projects consultant. She is the author of Jambalaya: The Natural Woman's Book of Personal Charms and Practical Rituals, Carnival of the Spirit, and Jump Up: Good Times Throughout the Season with Celebrations from Around the World. She is the Olori (director) of Ile Orunmila Oshun and the School of Ancient Mysteries/Sacred Arts Center in Oakland, Ca. She has taught at the University of Creation Spirituality- Naropa Oakland, John F. Kennedy University, The Institute for Transpersonal Psychology and New College of California.

Luisah Teish is an initiated elder (Iyanifa) in the Ifa/Orisha tradition of the West African Diaspora, and she holds a chieftaincy title (Yeye'woro) from the Fatunmise Compound in Ile Ife, Nigeria. Presently she is the Chair of the World Orisha Congress Committee on Women's Issues. She is also a devotee of Damballah Hwedo, the Haitian Rainbow Serpent, under the guidance of Moma Lola.

She was awarded a Ph.D. in Spiritual Therapeutics from Open International University's School of Complementary Medicine in Colombo Sri Lanka in 1993. She holds an Inter-Faith minister's license from the International Institute of Integral Human Sciences. In 1969 she received initiation into to the Fahamme Temple of Amun-Ra in St. Louis, Missouri.

Anniitra Makafia UtchatiNu Ravenmoon is a Priestess Hierophant of Fellowship of Isis, Founder of Iseum of the Nubian Moon, Daughter of Oya/Nekbet and Auset/Yemoja and Walking in the energy of Anubis Esu

Iyanifa Onifa Karade is an Ifa Priestess in the Yoruba tradition, voodooist, spiritualist, writer, and dreamer living in the Pacific Northwest USA.

Heaven Walker, also known as Lady Kahina, is the High Priestess of the "Sprouts" children's ritual circle of Come As You are coven. Heaven Walker is a High Priestess of both the Wildflower and Amazon traditions of Come As You Are Coven, the founder of the Grove of Artemis women's full moon circle, a priestess of the Corellian tradition, an initiate of the Gardnerian tradition, and a member of the Iseum of Black Isis. Heaven Walker is also a legally ordained interfaith minister who offers professional Tarot Card Readings, Spiritual Counseling, pagan and interfaith wedding ceremonies, and Rites of Passage.

Janet Callahan is a wife, mother, priestess, author, and artist living in the Detroit area. She has been published in the journal "Cup of Wonder" and in the book "Manifesting Prosperity: a Wealth Magick Anthology." You can read her thoughts on Pagan life, philosophy, and parenting at http://janetcallahan.com and http://ourlittleacorn.blogspot.com

Olivia Haynes, 23, resides in Baltimore, Maryland. She writes for alternative Black culture site Afro-Punk under the pen name "Black Witch" and soon will be publishing a book encompassing all her column entries in August, titled "Black Witch: Life from the Black Pagan Perspective". Essay "Why Don't You Like Me" is an entry included in the upcoming book. Black Witch is about life from the Black Pagan perspective.

Gloria Jean currently resides in northern California with her husband, two grown sons and two grandsons, as well as dogs and birds. She works as a legal assistant, though her passion is the Tarot, which she does professionally (www.Enchanted1Tarot.com). Gloria Jean works with many traditions and belief systems and will use her knowledge of world mythologies when preparing special petitions to the spirits on behalf of her clients.

Nadirah Adeye, MA, is an ordained Amazon priestess with over 15 years' experience in service to The Divine. She is a student priestess of the Iseum of Black Isis, a student of Feri, and is a devotee of Auset in Her many names and forms. Nadirah's spiritual work emphasizes self-mastery and contact with the Core energy found at the center of the world's most powerful and loving traditions.

Yonv Unega is a Pagan father living in California. He is a combination of mixed ancestry, including the blood of the Blackfoot and Cherokee tribes. He learned some of his beliefs from the teachings of his mother's druid practices and his grandmother's Native American blood. He works as a case manager with mentally ill, substance abusing and homeless adults in the Bay Area.

Szmeralda Shanel is an ordained priestess of Isis with the Temple of Isis and The Fellowship of Isis. She the founder of the Iseum of Black Isis, an iseum dedicated to Goddess spirituality and sacred arts. She is also an initiate in the Anderson Feri tradition, a high priestess in the Amazon Dianic Goddess tradition and one of the founding high priestesses of Come As You Are Coven. Outside the circle Szmeralda makes ends meet working as a teaching artist, an expressive arts therapist and tarot reader. www.blackisisiseum.com

Storm Kelly was born in a small town in southwestern Pennsylvania not far from Pittsburgh. She was always drawn to the mystical and supernatural energies since early childhood experiencing constant visions and paranormal activity. Her parents tried to hide these gifts and she was not permitted to speak of them. She eventually chose the Pagan path while in high school twenty years ago and has been on this path ever since. She did not have a teacher or mentor during her journey so throughout the years she has researched as much as she could on her own and adopted her own traditions. She currently resides in Ohio with her two teenage children and four furbabies. She enjoys paranormal investigations, reading, writing, and photography.

K.W. is a Black Witch following a Celtic path. She resides in the wilds of NYC. When not at her day job, you can find her with her nose in a book, practicing Welsh or dancing madly to Bollywood soundtracks.

Yvonne Nieves is a Chicago-native that specializes in marketing and public relations through her all-female company, Las Divas Promotions. She is a freelance writer, contributes regularly to The Offering Webzine and is a guest editor for Metal Alley Webzine. As a proud member of the Pagan community, Nieves is working with Witch School International's Pagans Tonight Blog Talk Radio team as an in-print and on-air news editor. She has formed a small circle of practicing light workers in Chicago's vibrant Pilsen neighborhood. A graduate of Northeastern Illinois University with a degree in Anthropology, Nieves has worked at The Field Museum of Natural History in Chicago working with cultural institutions throughout Chicagoland. She showcased her acting skills in the Chicago Latino Film Festival's Urban Poet and in the Chicago Center for Performing Arts' 2009 Brown Girls' Chronicles: Puerto Rican Women and Resilience. She is currently a student of the Hibiscus Moon Crystal Academy and in the process of obtaining her certification as a Crystal Healer with the World Metaphysical Association.

La PiXie (Sandra Posadas) is a Puerto Rican woman born and raised in Humboldt Park, Chicago, Illinois. She is a teacher, published artist and illustrator, artisan, performance poet and actor. La PiXie has been performing live since she was fourteen years old .She is an original cast member of the Vida Bella Ensemble, she successfully co-wrote her first production in 2007called Brown Girls Singing, staged at University of Chicago and Jane Addams' Hull House as part of Teatro Luna's Women of Color Playwriting Competition As a cast member of the Vida Bella Ensemble, she has also traveled to Colorado, California, and New York performing the award winning play, Brown Girls' Chronicles: Puerto Rican Women and Resilience. She participated as a cast member in Teatro Luna's 10 x10 Project. La PiXie's most recent performances projects include The Guild Complex's Poetry Performance Incubator series titled Tour Guides and Beast Woman Performance Series at The Green House Theater in Chicago. La PiXie has published her poetry in several anthologies including Stray Bullets: An Anthology of Chicago Saloon Poetry (Tia Chucha Press, 1990) and The Journal of Ordinary Thought (Fall 2009 and Winter 2009). She also performs at various Chicago venues and has presented her art work at several different local venues including The 2010 Logan Square Arts Festival, The University of Illinois at The Chicago Symposium for Women of Color, and The Creative Feminist Alliance at De Paul University. She was recently a featured poet with Proyecto Latina. La PiXie was also the winner and recipient of Tau Lambda Sorority's 1st Annual Salute to Latinas Poetry Competition in 2010.

La PiXie is not afraid to live life authentically and is all about telling it like is. She feels strongly that art can educate. She believes in using art as vehicle toward transformation so that all participants and spectators examine themselves in relation to their place in society. Through the variety of modalities that she uses to transmit her messages, whether it is visual or interactive, the audience may explore, reflect, analyze and transform the realities in which they live.

Lilith Silverkrow (Erica L. Gordon) is a Certified Shamanic Soul Coach, a Core Shaman, Priestess and Witch. Currently residing in the Local Portland area, Lilith teaches classes, and does Shamanic Soul Coaching, Intuitive readings, and legal rights of passages.

In 2005, Lilith Moved to California, where she would begin her journey into Shamanism, from then, she was called to move to Portland to fulfill her dream of becoming a community leader, providing services to the community. Lilith is also a Kundalini Reiki Master, and teacher of the Craft, and is on the continuous path of a spiritual student. Lilith is the founder of New Pagan Journeys Community Learning Center in the Tigard, Oregon Area.

Uzuri Amini (Ishe Fa'lona Oshun Iya Oshogbo) is an initiated priest of Oshun, the Yoruba goddess of love, healing and art; as well as a writer, artist and ceremonialist. She has contributed to several anthologies, notably *The Goddess Celebrates; Earthwalking Sky Dancers; A Waist is a Terrible Thing to Mind; Talking to the Goddess*; and the *Festival of the Bones Series, Books 1 & 2*. She is also a member of the International Women's Writing Guild and the Elder's Council of Ile Orunmila Oshun (for 21 years) and core faculty of the School of Ancient Mysteries/Sacred Arts Center directed by Luisah Teish in Oakland, CA.

Faith Bond, aka Flame Bridhesdottir, is a very married, middle aged, stay at home mother of four and a self described "Serpent Child of the Universe." Unable to point to any actual achievements, she is better known for her inappropriate humor, wildly fluctuating waistline, and abhorrence of the wilfully ignorant. Flame can frequently be seen standing in her backyard shaking her fists at the sky. She grudgingly resides in Ohio with her husband and children and one insane orange tabby.

Luna Pantera: Part of my life's work is helping others heal from the pain of rape, incest, and domestic violence. As a witch I know the sacredness of Sexuality and the significance it has in our life as a connecting force to Deity and our higher selves. I use my gifts as an intuitive healer, witch, seer, and Reiki practitioner to help my clients reconnect with their core self. The piece "Tapestry of the Soul" was written after a vision I was gifted with by Oshun at a spiritual retreat I had been attending. The narrative helped me put into words my own experience and is offered as a way to *"break the silence"*that exists in my community and all communities that sacrifice the soul and will being of their girls and woman for the self esteem and false facade of their males. And more importantly it shows the healing that can occur when we work with Spirit! Let the healing continue; let the healing begin!!!

Leilani Birely is a Hawaiian Priestess and ceremonialist, brings ancient Hawaiian healing and Goddess wisdom to the community. She is the active mother of two girls. Graduated from George Mason University in Fairfax VA with a degree in Business, and a graduate of the Masters in Womyn's Spirituality from New College in San Francisco. On Summer solstice of 1996 she founded Daughters of the Goddess Womyn's Temple. In August of 1998, she was Ordained as a Dianic High Priestess by Z Budapest at the Goddess 2000 womyn's Festival in La Honda, CA. For more information please see our website at DaughtersoftheGoddess.com.